The Inviting Church

a study of new member assimilation

Roy M. Oswald and Speed B. Leas

Research from The Alban Institute

The Publications Program of The Alban Institute is assisted by a grant from Trinity Church, New York City.

Library of Congress Catalog Card #87-71965.

TABLE OF CONTENTS

ACKNOWLEDGMENTS

In addition to acknowledging the generous contributions from the foundations and funders mentioned in the introduction, especially the Veatch Foundation, The Trinity Church Foundation, and the J. C. Penney Foundation, the authors extend their sincere thanks to all the people who helped to bring this project into reality.

This book is the joint effort of three people on the Alban Institute staff: Bob Gribbon, Roy Oswald and Speed Leas. Bob did the background research, and wrote a very useful paper,[1] which contributed significantly to this report. Roy and Speed trained the interviewers, supervised their work, helped analyze the information they collected, and put together this book.

We are also grateful to the Reverend Mr. George Regas, rector of All Saints Episcopal Church in Pasadena, California, who brought to our attention the paper written for his congregation by Rick Thyne and Neil Clark Warren. We appreciate very much their willingness to share this plan, and to allow us to reprint it as an example of how one church has taken the assimilation process seriously.

We are most grateful for the consultants who gave prodigious amounts of time freely to do the legwork for this project, for the churches and their pastors who allowed us to come into their congregations and shared their lives with us, and for the newcomers who eagerly shared their journeys into their new congregation.

The consultants who worked with us in Atlanta were Kathleen Bates, Brenda Birdsey, Herbert Burt, Marie Cochran, Jane Cocking, Grace Ann Collins, Barbara Coplin, John Faircloth, Shirley Ford-Adams, Betty Lee Hudson, Joel Hudson, Janice Johnson Hume, Knob Knobel, Mary Nell McLauchlin, Elizabeth McMaster, Jane Moser, Eileen Motter, and Ray Woods.

The consultants who worked with us in Philadelphia were: E. Marie Boyle, The Reverend Ned Castner, The Reverend Lois Goodman, The Reverend Judy M. Kehler, The Reverend David Lewis, The Reverend William Thomas Martin, Betty Metzler, The Reverend Gordon E. Simmons, Patricia L. Smith, Karen F. Snow, The Reverend David Thomas, Joan Vassar-Williams, and Janet A. Waechter.

And, of course, thanks to Celia Hahn, Director of Publications, who has patiently worked with us as we missed deadlines and changed material. We gratefully acknowledge our debt, and the debt of the Alban Institute to her leadership and support.

Speed Leas
Roy Oswald

1. Bob Gribbon, *"What Helps Churches Grow?"*, (Washington: The Alban Institute, Inc., 1984). This is a background paper for Assimilating New Members Research Project, sponsored by the Veatch Program. The factors affecting churches are taken from *Understanding Church Growth and Decline*, edited by Dean R. Hoge and David A. Roozen (Pilgrim, 1979.) (On Demand Publication, duplicated on request for members.)

Since its beginning, the Alban Institute has been interested in how people discover, get in, and stay in the local church. In 1980 and 1981 Roy Oswald conducted a study of six Episcopal congregations in Indiana and Maryland, with the help of Alice B. Mann, Jill Hudson and Robert T. Gribbon.[1]

We sent two interviewers into each of the six congregations to study newcomers' experiences in discovering, getting in and growing in those local churches. The study as much whetted our appetites for more learning as it provided insight into some of the common experience of new arrivals in an Episcopal Church. Out of this study, Roy wrote up some of his learning, and then conducted several seminars around the country based on these findings. Alice wrote a book on the incorporation of new members into the church.[2]

Because of the new interest stimulated by this earlier research, we wrote a proposal to the Veatch Foundation, associated with the North Shore Unitarian Universalist Church in Plandome, New York. The Foundation generously supplied us enough money to study eight congregations in each of two metropolitan areas in the Eastern part of the United States. We chose Atlanta and Philadelphia.

We invited approximately sixteen consultants each from Atlanta and Philadelphia to be trained in interviewing techniques. After they were trained, consulting teams of two went to congregations we had selected to interview thirty newcomers, the church staff, and a few key leaders about the experience newcomers had in that congregation and the experience the congregation intended them to have. When the interviews were complete the consultants wrote a report for the leaders of the congregation about its assimilation processes. After reviewing the report some of the congregations contracted with the consultants for further assistance. The report was shared with the Alban Institute, as well.

For this research we wanted churches of various sizes which were representative of a variety of denominations located in stable communities. Our hope was that we might notice some factors that were "causing" growth which were intrinsic to the congregations, as distinguished from "external" factors—like being located in a growing community. By and large we were successful at locating growing churches in stable communities. However, our sample was not as representative with regard to size as we might have hoped. We had no family-sized congregations (less than 50 attending Sunday morning) in the study. The denominations which were included in the study were: Lutheran, United Methodist, Unitarian, Episcopal, and Presbyterian.

But studying congregations was not the only way we went about pulling material together for this manuscript. We reviewed some of the literature on church growth and assimilation of members. And, in the role of consultants to local churches, we have worked with members on assimilation systems. We have encouraged congregations to try "shepherding programs," to set up systems for identifying and contacting newcomers, to train their members to call on and "recruit" new members, and so on—with varying results.

This book is a compendium of these various experiences: reading, research, and consulting.

The Purpose of this Book

The purpose of this book is to share with you our reflections on what happens to people as they discover, explore, and then join a local congregation. Some of what we will have to say here is *descriptive* of our experience and what we have heard newcomers say about what befell them as they moved into a congregation. In other parts of this book you will find that what we have to say is *prescriptive*, that is, we will suggest some things that have been useful to leaders in developing processes to assist newcomers as they discover, explore, and then join a local congregation. We have also been surprised by some things that *don't* seem to help much in assimilating people into the church.

The Outline of the Book

The book is organized around categories of experience relevant to leaders of congregations who are interested in helping people find their way into and become a part of a local church.

The first chapter helps the reader reflect on the fact that much of what affects growth and assimilation is outside the control of the leadership of the congregation. Population trends, demographic factors, and denominational identity are powerful influences on growth patterns in a congregation. Church leadership should have some sense of what is happening that they can do something about, and what is happening over which they have little or no control.

In the second chapter we examine what goes on inside the congregation. What kind of a place is it that people are being attracted to (or not being attracted to)? In our research we found that the congregation's sense of mission and its internal life will also affect who comes to the church and who stays.

The third chapter is an extension of the second. Here we look at the varying dynamics of congregations according to their size. Arlin Rothauge has been our mentor here and we draw heavily on his seminal contributions to understanding assimilation into congregations based on differentiating them according to size.

Chapters four through seven explore the "stages" of experience one is likely to have when "joining" a church. We take the reader through the newcomer's experiences, from first awareness that the church exists, to walking into the building, to formally joining and then going deeper into the Christian faith journey.

Our final chapter reviews how a congregational leader might bring these growth and assimilation issues to the attention of other leaders in the church, including the clergy and the church board.

Doing this research, reading the literature relevant to this topic, and writing this book has been an exciting and fulfilling journey for us. We have learned a little more about churches. We have learned a little more about people. We have learned a little more about Christians. We share our learnings with you in the hope that they will further your enthusiasm for the church and stimulate your participation in its growth and development.

NOTES—INTRODUCTION

1. This study was funded by The Episcopal Diocese of Indiana, St. Paul's Episcopal Church in Indianapolis, The J. C. Penney Foundation, Trinity Church, Wall Street, and The Alban Institute, Inc.

2. Alice Mann, *Incorporation of New Members in the Episcopal Church: A Manual for Clergy and Lay Leaders*, (Philadelphia: Ascension Press, 1983).

CHAPTER I

Church Growth and Factors Outside the Control of the Congregation

When we look at how people find and join a church most of us tend to focus on those things that we can do something about. We look at the quality of our life in the congregation. We look at the recruiting that is being done and not being done. We look at the processes that make the newcomer feel welcome or alienated, lost or at home. However, focusing on these factors may give us a distorted picture of what is at work when new people are finding their way into a congregation. Much that affects the numbers of people showing up and exploring the possibility of joining a congregation is not within the control of the church members. Some of the factors that affect the rate at which newcomers show up are a part of the dynamic of what is happening in our culture as a whole (especially with regard to participation in institutionalized religion), or a part of trends in particular denominations (some denominations are growing faster than others—and some are declining). Other factors that have to do with the part of the country in which the church is located, and what is happening demographically in the neighborhood in which a particular church is located. Bob Gribbon has done some interesting and very helpful research on these factors from which we are drawing and quoting heavily here.[1] Gribbon points to three areas outside the control of the congregation, which, nevertheless, affect church attendance. He calls them National Contextual Factors, National Denominational Factors, and Local Contextual Factors. We will briefly explore each in turn.

National Contextual Factors

Overall, says Gribbon, churches in the US still operate in a culturally favorable context. Support for the local church remains strong. In an average week, 41 percent of adult Americans attend worship services. Despite declines in the public confidence in institutions, "organized religion" leads the list of institutions in which Americans have "a great deal" of confidence. Americans are far more likely than Europeans or Japanese to say that religion is important to them and to say that they are "a religious person." Eighty-six percent of American adults say that religion is "very" or "fairly" important to them; eighty-one percent define themselves as "a religious person." Ninety-five percent of adult Americans say that they believe in God.

However, all is not rosy out there. As a percentage of the population the Protestant majority is declining. In 1952 Protestants were 67 percent of the population; in the '80s we are 57 percent. This is a proportional loss of 15 percent.[2] And there is clearly a pattern of decline, especially among younger people, in religious participation in moderate and liberal denominations. Roof and McKinney expect that among all the churches the Protestant establishment will continue to lose ground both in social power and influence:

> Birth cohorts tell the story. Most of the moderate-to-liberal denominations have lost ground among the recently born. Methodists, for example, often viewed as the most representative American religious group, made up 16 percent of all Americans born around the turn of the century but only 7.7 of those born between 1958 and 1965. Despite the new growth of Methodism's churches during the twentieth century, its "market share" declined by about one-half. Similar shrinkage has occurred for Lutherans, Presbyterians, Episcopalians, the United Church of Christ, and the Unitarian-Universalists. The low birth rates of these groups are largely responsible for the declines. A small rate of natural growth combined with fewer gains from inter-denominational switching in the post-1960s era have given them a weakened demographic base. Overall, the evidence seems irrefutable: the liberal branches of Protestantism are shrinking both as a proportion of Protestantism and of the general public.[3]

It is fascinating to observe that the changes in the birthrate seem to correlate with changes in the church-going rate. In the Eisenhower era the birthrate was high nationally and it was a prosperous time for the religious establishment. The birthrate declined significantly in the 60s and it has not gone up again.

When one looks at the figures on church attendance, one can see that they dramatically increased in the years after World War II, accompanying the increase in the rate of family formation and the boom of new communities and new churches in the suburbs. From a high point in the late 1950's, the church attendance rate has declined. One needs not to become depressed over these figures, in

that since 1969 the percentage of adults attending church in a typi-
cal week has not varied more than two percent annually (though
most of that change in attendance has been downward).

The New Volunteerism

"The New Volunteerism" is a phrase used by Roof and McKinney to
describe what has been happening recently in our culture that
seems to contribute to the diminishing commitment to religious institutions in general. They describe this new religious volunteerism
as a quest for self-fulfillment, movement away from older religious
norms of self-denial and toward norms of self-gratification and en-
joyment as ends in themselves. The impact of this new religious volunteerism has three dimensions which Roof and McKinney
describe. First, there is a new emphasis on religion as individual experience, a quest for personal authenticity and a sense of wholeness
which takes people out of churches and into their own spiritual or-
bits. "Salvation is identical with fulfillment, something that could
only be found 'within' the self—and perhaps best outside organized
religion."[4] The second dimension is the emphasis on emancipation
of the self. Individuals believe that to find their true selves they
must be freed of any obstacles standing in their way. Thus social
roles, status, and religious duty have lost much of their authority as
individuals seek authentic identities outside of established institutions or from only partially within them. The third dimension is that
of the autonomous individual against the institution! Religious institutions should serve individuals, and not vice versa.

   This new religious volunteerism means individuals are more
likely to stand back from churches and ask what these institutions
can do for them. People are less likely to join out of a loyalty to
family values and identities or values based on old ethnic group or
social class loyalties than has been the case in the past. "Under less
pressure to adhere to old group loyalties, persons are free to make
decisions on the basis of genuine *religious* preference. With con-
formity less of an influence, religious inclination itself becomes
more of a factor."[5]

The Baby Boomers

While the overall context for church attendance is getting mixed reviews, the baby boomers are bringing increasing numbers of people into churches for the short term. To understand this
phenomenon it is important to understand the stages of participation through which most people in this culture seem to go as they
mature from the teen years into adulthood. Young people 18 to 25
years of age (Gribbon calls these people transitional young adults)

are less likely than any other age group to attend church. Transitional young adults are explorers of the world. They seldom lose their faith but their behavior changes. At this age young adults are most likely to be critical of religious institutions and have negative images of organized religion. However, they report high levels of belief in God and concern for religious and philosophical ideals. People of this age group move more often than any other group in the population. Gribbon says that this period of "dropping out" of church lasts for about eight years.

In their late twenties adults begin to become more settled. They make some decisions about career, marriage, and life style. These choices may not be fixed for life, but they yield a greater sense of identity. These young adults know who they are and how they fit into the world. The median age for women in their first marriage is 23 and it is 25 for men.

The period of "return" to church begins in the late twenties, usually before the age of 30. The average age of return is 26-27. What are the characteristics of these young people that are relevant to church attendance?

The reasons for returning to church seem to be mostly unconscious; according to Levinson, this era in an individual's life seems to be a time when people have a need for "rooting." They are extending or building a stable life structure. This is a "settling" period—especially for their private or personal life, not necessarily their work life. It is likely that people at this age are becoming more conservative than they were a few years previously.

People who are "returning" to church are likely to have a child—or are about to have one. But it is difficult to make a case that they are really going to church "for" the children; more likely, says Gribbon, they are going for themselves and find it easier to talk about the children's needs than their own. They certainly do not stay for the sake of the children. They stay if they get what they are looking for as adults.

At this time, in terms of the national context, then, we have an especially large group of people who would "naturally" be coming back to church at the age of between 26 and 32; and with the "Baby Boom" we have an exceptionally large group of people of this age now in our culture. The existence of this large particularly "ripe" group for new church membership provides a favorable situation for churches in that large numbers of "young people" are likely to be "coming back" to church. This will be a time when the church's receptivity and ability to assimilate them into the life of the congregation will be tested.

The church's job is not an easy one. As we have pointed out above, the people who are returning to church seem to have values

and cultural characteristics which are dissimilar to those now in the
majority in the congregations they will joining. This younger generation puts a greater emphasis on self-fulfillment than has been the
case for those who are older. Further the younger people have a
greater tolerance for diversity of lifestyles than the previous generation. However, it should be noted that while the Baby Boomers are
more liberal than those they are joining in church, this does not
mean that they are as liberal as those who do not join. Those who
do not attend any church tend to be the most liberal; the young
people who attend church are less conservative than those who are
already members and more conservative than their peers who stay
away.

Further, Baby Boomers have fewer institutional commitments
than those who preceded them. They join what satisfies and drop
out of that which does not. Divorce rates (though they are again
improving) may be another symptom of this decreased commitment. The ease with which younger people change denominations
is another illustration of the same point. Thus, Baby Boomers do
not have the same values as those who are now in charge of the
congregations the young people are joining. Current congregational
leaders have a high value for loyalty and commitment and tend to
be disdainful of people who "shop" for churches or church programs to meet their own personal needs.

These value and life-style differences are going to make assimilation difficult. In order for the assimilation to "take" it will be necessary for the persons involved (both members and newcomers) to
listen to one another, to have compassion for other perspectives,
and to negotiate creative ways of programming and functioning so
that differences can be enjoyed, or least become opportunities for
growth and learning rather than dissatisfaction and pain.

National Denominational Factors

What happens to and in local churches is not just a function of what
is happening in the culture at large. Denominational experience
and culture seem to have an impact on whether a church will grow
and how rapidly it will grow.

Some denominations grow faster than others. The old mainline
denominations such as Episcopalians, Congregationalists, Presbyterians, Methodists and Unitarians have shown similar patterns of decline. At the same time, Southern Baptists and other evangelical or
conservative churches have shown patterns of growth.

It has been suggested that many people left the more "liberal" churches because of their positions on social issues, but this has not been shown to be the case. Apparently, people do not leave the more "liberal" churches for the more "conservative" on any widespread basis. In fact, if there is a trend for leaving one denomination to join another, the largest trend is for people to switch "up" the sociological ladder into the mainline denominations. Those who leave the more liberal churches seem to leave churches altogether.

There are other reasons why attendance in mainline denominations is declining. They draw more of their members from the upper socioeconomic brackets that have been most influenced by the value shifts taking place in our society, especially those shifts away from church participation.

Further, this group has had a lower birthrate and thus has replaced fewer members by "biological growth." The strength of the mainline denominations has been drawn from Americans of northern European extraction, and this group is declining as a percentage of the U.S. population. Moreover, the strength of many of the mainline denominations has been in areas of stable or declining population such as the northeastern states and central cities—another factor which clearly hinders the probability of church growth.

To understand why the declining denominations are declining and the growing ones are growing it might be instructive to look at the Southern Baptist and the Assemblies of God denominations. The Southern Baptists increased 1.16 percent in 1984, the Assemblies of God 2.19 percent, while the mainline churches dropped in membership. The smallest mainline decline was in the Lutheran Church Missouri-Synod with a .11 percent drop. The largest was .69 percent in The Episcopal Church.[6]

Why are the Southern Baptists and Assemblies of God growing? Part of the reason certainly lies in their location and the culture of their churches. Their strength has been in the Southern states which have been experiencing rapid population growth while maintaining a relatively stable culture conducive to church growth. The regional cultural style of the South still includes the highest rate of church membership and attendance. At the same time, denominational policies make a difference. These denominations have traditionally placed more emphasis on "soul winning" than some other traditions. Further, they have intentionally reached out to new populations. An example of the result of this policy is the fact that new Southern Baptist congregations with ethnic minorities are being started in an area in which the more mainline American Baptist church is declining.

The culture of the denominations themselves with regard to institutional commitment makes a difference as well, as you can see from the following table.[7] The numbers in the columns represent the percentage of people who responded to questions about their religious participation. "How often do you attend religious services?" Thirty-four percent of the sample attend less than once or twice a year; 21 percent were occasional attenders; and 46 percent attended nearly every week or more often. Denominational commitment was measured with the question "Would you call yourself a strong [Presbyterian]?" Overall, 43 percent of the sample consider themselves "strong" members.

Religious Participation of Religious Groups

| | Church Attendance | | | High Denom'l |
	Low	Moderate	Regular	Commitment
National	34	21	46	43
Liberal Protestants	37	24	39	33
Episcopalians	39	28	33	32
United Church of Christ	32	24	44	39
Presbyterians	37	22	40	32
Moderate Protestants	35	23	41	36
Methodists	38	24	38	32
Lutherans	29	26	45	41
Christians	30	19	51	50
(Disciples of Christ)				
Northern Baptists	44	19	37	34
Reformed	25	12	64	59
Black Protestants	20	25	56	52
Methodists	17	26	57	58
Northern Baptists	27	27	46	46
Southern Baptists	15	23	62	55
Conservative Protestants	24	19	58	53
Southern Baptists	26	22	52	48
Churches of Christ	19	19	62	57
Evangelicals/				
Fundamentalists	18	5	77	63
Nazarenes	24	12	64	63
Pentecostals/Holiness	19	16	65	58
Assemblies of God	16	11	73	70
Churches of God	31	12	57	59
Adventists	24	13	63	59
Catholics	25	20	55	42
Jews	48	39	13	42
Others				
Mormons	27	9	64	59
Jehovah's Witnesses	13	10	77	58
Christian Scientists	31	25	44	40
Unitarian-Universalists	64	14	22	35
No religious preference	91	6	3	—

Obviously the culture of a denomination will affect the ease with which people leave a congregation (and perhaps the ease with which they join) as well as the level of their participation.

Local Contextual Factors

Yet the two most powerful factors affecting church growth and decline of a particular congregation are neither national external nor denominational external factors. They are neighborhood contextual factors—that is, factors that shape the quality of life in the neighborhood in which the church is located—and local institutional factors—that is, the quality of life within the congregation. In comparing neighborhood contextual factors with local institutional factors the contextual factors seemed to account for 56% of the variance between growing and non-growing congregations and 44% seemed to be accounted for by local institutional factors, say Roof, Hoge, Dyble, and Hadaway.[8]

> The issue is not really one set of factors versus the other, but rather the conditions under which one or the other predominates in influence, or how the two together explain trends neither can account for alone.[9]

These authors[10] list a number of factors in the community which do affect church growth:

Affluence

Older homes near church	Negative Correlation
Older church building	Negative Correlation
Economic level of people near church	Positive Correlation
Higher percent renters near church	Negative Correlation

Demographic Change

Increase in school population	Positive Correlation
Increase in economic level	Positive Correlation
Increase in older persons	Slight Negative Correlation
Increase in younger persons	Slight Positive Correlation
Increase in minorities	Small Negative Correlation
Increase in families	Small Positive Correlation
Increase in newcomers	Slight Positive Correlation
Increase in Protestants	Slight Positive Correlation

Community Facilities

Location near church of banks	Slight Negative Correlation
Location near retail stores	Slight Negative Correlation
Location near church of farms	Slight Positive Correlation
Location near public schools	Slight Negative Correlation

Community Type

Suburb versus city/town/country	Slight Positive Correlation
Suburb/town/country versus city	Small Positive Correlation

Church Competition

Other Protestant churches near	Small Negative Correlation

Those factors which most significantly affect the growth of a congregation are outside the congregation's direct control. They include increasing affluence in the community in which the church is located—such factors as newer homes near the church and an increasing income of the people who live near the church. They have to do with demographic change in the neighborhood as well—an increase in the number of families in the area, an increasing school population, an increasing Protestant population. Decreasing congregations seem to be in areas where affluence is decreasing, renters are increasing, and the population density is increasing.

Put in the words of those who did the research:

> . . .demographic change (with all else controlled) accounts for eight percent of the variance, and affluence (with all else controlled) accounts for four percent. None of the other clusters accounts for over one percent. The conclusion is quite clear: *affluence* and *demographic change* are the best overall predictors of church growth among all these factors. Hypotheses concerning these factors receive greater support than do hypotheses about community type, institutions and facilities, or church competition.[11]

When one puts these two factors together statistically they account for a little more than 14 percent of that which affects growth.[12] It needs to be noted that *no factors* have overwhelming influence on whether a church will grow or not. Demographic change, which is the most significant factor, accounts for only eight percent of the change. To keep in perspective what we are talking about here, one would not want to see his or her situation as hopeless just because the number of renters is increasing or there is an overall decrease in income in the community. These negative factors will make the job of attracting and recruiting new people more difficult, but not overwhelming.

What these statistics give us is information about what we are up against; they do not predict success or failure of a particular congregation's ability to assimilate members or to grow. Further, it does not seem to us that the task of the church is always to be successful; rather it is to be faithful, which means that one stays true to the call of Christ to make disciples of all people, *and it means that one understands that success has different standards in different settings.*

So mainline congregations will be helped to hold their own and grow by many factors in the community in which they are located and in our culture. Some of these factors are:

> The generally positive value of church attendance in the culture
> The birth rate which rose after World War II
> The need of younger people for "rooting".
> Rising affluence in the community in which the church is located
> Increasing numbers of people with children moving into the community.

But there are many factors also which will inhibit this growth:

> The small, but steady decline in mainline church participation in the culture at large
> The changing values of the culture of the Baby Boomers which may constrain their inclusion fully into the church
> The diminished need this new generation has to be loyal and committed to institutions
> The aging of the church and the community around it (including the homes and the people)
> An increase in the number of renters in the area around the church.

NOTES—CHAPTER I

1. Bob Gribbon, "What Helps Churches Grow," (The Alban Institute, Inc., 1984). This is a background paper for the Assimilating New Members Research Project, sponsored by the Veatch Program.
2. Wade Clark Roof and William McKinney, *American Mainline Religion: Its Changing Shape and Future*, (New Brunswick: Rutgers University Press, p. 15).
3. ibid., p. 234.
4. ibid., p. 50.
5. ibid., p. 69.

6. Quoted in "Events and People," *The Christian Century*, August 13-20, 1986, p. 705.

7. Roof and McKinney, Op. cit., pp. 83-84.

8. Wade Clark Roof, Dean R. Hoge, John E. Dyble and C. Kirk Hadaway, "Factors Producing Growth or Decline in United Presbyterian Congregations," ed. Dean R. Hoge and David Roozen, *Understanding Church Growth and Decline*, (New York: The Pilgrim Press, 1979, p. 222).

9. ibid.

10. ibid, p. 208.

11. ibid, p. 212.

12. ibid, p. 220.

CHAPTER II

Church Growth and Factors Within the Control of the Congregation

Having reviewed some of the factors affecting the possibilities for church growth outside the congregation's control, we now turn to an overview of those factors which are more (though not entirely) within the control of the congregation. These aspects of the congregational situation over which the congregation has more control have been called by Roof, Hoge, Dyble, and Hadaway, "institutional factors" (or factors within the life of the congregation as opposed to environmental or contextual factors). The inside and outside factors seem to have fairly equal influences on growth patterns. Community contextual factors described in the last chapter combined to account for about 56 percent of impact on growth; and the institutional factors 44 percent. Quoting from Roof, Hoge, Dyble, and Hadaway:

> Among the institutional cluster, only three have much overall impact: satisfaction with worship and program, social action involvement, and congregational harmony and cooperation. Worship and program satisfaction is very important, accounting for about one half the variance explained by institutional factors. Congregational harmony and cooperation is the second most important cluster, followed by social involvement. These three explain 11.4 percent of the variance above and beyond that accounted for by the contextual factors, thus comprising about 44 percent of the total explained variance.[1]

Listed according to the relative importance of institutional factors in relationship to growth, these researchers found the following factors to be significantly correlated to church growth:

Satisfaction with Church Worship and Program
Congregational Harmony and Cooperation (disunity was associated with decline)
Social Action

The Pastor
Small Group Activities

These statistical analyses relate to that which is associated with growth or decline in congregations—that is, the number of people enrolling in congregations. The research which provided the impetus for this report was not focused strictly on the issue of church growth. For the most part we chose for our research congregations that were growing. Thus, it would be likely that these congregations would not be experiencing much disunity (and this was the case).

We expected to find a high degree of satisfaction with the church worship and program (and this was the case). We have included this introductory material here because we want to set the discussion of those factors which affect assimilation in the appropriate context. We assumed that churches which were growing, but were not located in areas where the community contextual factors would have had significant impact on the number of people joining them, might have something special going on in them that would help them grow despite the fact that the environmental factors were not also helping them. In choosing churches that were growing we assumed they had some competence at assimilation, assuming that growth could be attributed to something other than demographic change.

Based on the experience of the researchers in this Alban Institute project, the factors we identified that helped most with the attraction, introduction, and inclusion of new members into the life of a congregation were

a positive identity
congregational harmony
the pastor's ability to generate enthusiasm
the congregation's involvement in social action or social service
small group programming.

This list is very close to that generated earlier by the authors of the research quoted above.

A Positive Identity

What struck us most profoundly in our research is that those churches which we studied had almost no formal assimilation systems whatsoever! For the most part what happened to help people become members was informal, unplanned, unsupervised, and un-intentional.

Most books about managing churches say that if you want to grow you should have an assimilation process which is clear, planned, agreed on, with trained volunteers and without gaps in helping the newcomer move from the outside of the church into its center. Though all that sounds like a great idea, from our work with these sixteen "successful" congregations we found that high commitment to an organized assimilation process was not the hallmark of the congregations we studied.

What seems to be more important than anything else is that growing congregations have a positive personality which showed through in the church's (a) energy, (b) belief in inclusion, and (c) sense of having a unique identity.

Energy

Universally, our consultants found that those churches we studied had an *elan*, an animating force, that moved people. They were not still; they were not dull. Activity seemed to characterize the place, and not just on Sunday morning. People were there throughout the week and they were involved in something—running the church, cleaning it up, studying the Bible, praying, helping others—you name it. These congregations were not places to which you escape. They demanded something of you; they demanded your time, your involvement, your participation, your enthusiasm. The members seemed to vibrate when they got together, and they set the new-comers to vibrating as well; so that the newcomers were looking for ways to get in—whether the congregation made the way easy for them or not. And many times the members of the congregation did not make it easy for the new arrivals to get in. One person who had joined her church about a year before she was interviewed by us said, "You have to fight your way into this church. It's not that they want to keep you out or they are indifferent, rather they are so into what they are doing that they don't seem to really notice you and help you find your place here."

A Belief in Inclusion

This was an interesting discovery in our research. We found that the churches really didn't do very much to help people get in. Most of them did have greeters on Sunday morning, and a couple had committees of people that were supposed to "follow-up" on people who came to church more than a couple of times; but even those churches that had these committees didn't do what they were set up

to do. In other words, the people who still felt like guests in the
church had little or nothing happen to them that would help them

Get to know other members
Find a group in which they might be interested in participating
Find the church office, or rest room, or nursery
Discover what services (worship and helping) the church of-
    fered
Learn what one has to do to become a member
Tell others about who they are.

Nonetheless, these churches *believed* in inclusion. They saw
themselves as friendly, open, interested in newcomers, wanting others to be included in what they were doing and to share in the excitement of being a member of this religious community. When the
churches were given feedback on the fact that very little was done
to help people get in, members acknowledged that more could be
done. But they were surprised that very little was happening. They
believed they were doing a great deal to help people feel at home
and find their way into the life of the church.

It may be that belief in inclusion is a powerful magnet that is
non-verbally (or non-directly) transmitted to the newcomer. The
new person, perhaps subliminally, gets the message, "We want you;
we would like you to be a part of our fellowship," even though
there was no greeter or official body to come right out and say it.

Identity

Members of growing churches think that they are special, unique,
not like anyone else. They have a "strength at the center," a basic
integrity or vigor at the center of parish life. In short, the congregation offers something of substance to people. That substance
matches the basic human hunger within people seeking a church
family.

The message the church proclaims is central to this identity.
When it knows that its basic enterprise is to proclaim a message of
faith, hope, and love to the world, and it is doing it, it feeds its people with bread and not a stone. No amount of propaganda or organization will cover a lack of substance at the core. It is folly for
congregations to work at improving their incorporation process
when they do not have substantial food to nourish people once
they are incorporated. It's like putting whipped cream on stale pud-
ding.

In the churches we studied, the job of proclamation did not fall
solely on clergy or totally on the Sunday morning worship experi-

ence. The members also felt the burden and privilege of proclaiming good news to each other.

These congregations didn't have gimmicks to get people there and keep them in. They had a revitalizing spirit that extended throughout the membership of the congregation which was visible in the relationship between the members and their pastor.

What is identity? It is the "we" that endures through the shifting styles and circumstances of the congregation, that persists through the loss of members as well as the addition of new ones. Erikson defined identity as "accrued confidence." It is the result of communication among members through which they share perceptions of themselves, their church and their world. It includes the values that they have in common and the agreed-upon means by which they interact. It includes their common vision or goal as well as the flavor or style that they have developed as institutions over the years. It is the attraction one feels to "my kind of people;" it is the hope we have of what we can become.[2]

As a church develops an identity, it will find itself with "boundaries"; that is, it will be saying "no" to some activities and to some people, and "yes" to others. It is not possible to be a healthy institution without boundaries. Or as Lyle Schaller would ask, "Who do you exclude?" A Christian church usually excludes people who do not profess belief in Jesus as Lord. When the church says "believers are the kind of people we want," they are excluding those who are not believers—or at least those who are not interested in exploring the possibility of belief. Most members would feel comfortable with this boundary: "We are a community of people who profess this belief about God and the way God is revealed to us." But there are other boundaries that help us differentiate between "us" and "notus." For example, some churches "exclude" those who are not comfortable with a certain kind of theology or those within certain economic brackets (high as well as low). Some churches exclude certain ethnic groups, others exclude those who don't include several ethnic groups (in other words, those who are not committed to keeping an integrated congregation), and so on.

Boundaries are needed for a healthy identity. If the church doesn't know who it is, if it doesn't know who belongs here—or doesn't agree on who should belong—the invitations, the reaching out to others will be half-hearted and not convincing. When we know who we are, what we are here for, we are then able to attract and integrate (assimilate) people into a community. Those who don't know who they are, what they are there for, or what they are doing will not be sure why they are asking others to join and will very likely communicate (subliminally), "You probably wouldn't want to be one of us anyway, but we need more bodies and more money around here, and we certainly would appreciate the help."

It should be noted in this context that the argument presented by Dean Kelley in *Why Conservative Churches Are Growing*[3] that conservative churches are more likely to grow the higher they are on the "Exclusivist-Ecumenical Gradient" seems also to support this point. Kelley's point is that those churches which are most separate or distinct from the mainstream culture seem to have the best chance of growing. Those most like the mainstream culture "will tend to diminish in numbers." Other research and literature reflecting on this point make the same point just as boldly. Roof and McKinney say that "the plight of the liberal Protestant churches is. . .a lack of cohesion, too much openness and diffuseness, and absence of any clear sense of institutional identity."[4] Roof and McKinney argue that

> A crucial challenge for liberal Protestantism is to recapture some sense of particularity as a community of memory and not merely as a custodian of generalized cultural values. This will require among other things a countering of the secular drift that has had a disproportionate impact on its traditional constituency. The liberal churches need their own particular language of faith to communicate with the "cultured despisers" of the modern world, in a manner that lays claim upon the self and the community.
>
> This task will not be easy. As we have shown, in the past two decades the liberal churches have not lost members to the conservative churches, but to the ranks of the nonaffiliated and the "unchurched." Liberal Protestantism's "competition" is not the conservatives it has *spurned* but the secularists it has *spawned.* This latter group includes the most liberal segments of the population, people unlikely to join the ranks of the hard-line conservatives. Liberal Protestantism's future, we believe, lies not in a move toward the theological and ideological right, but in its becoming more self-consciously "liberal," if by that is meant an assertion of responsible individualism in a communal framework. If these churches are to reclaim the loyalties of persons lost to this secular-minded constituency, they will need to hold firm to their historic values and to testify to them in as direct and forceful manner as possible.[5]

Perhaps the reader does not agrees that his or her church should become "more self-consciously liberal." Indeed, that may create more disharmony in the congregation than would be healthy for growth and assimilation. However, the point made by Roof and McKinney is important and well taken. The church must discover what it is called to be and then self-consciously work to fulfill that ministry.

Examples of Churches with Clear Identity

One of the congregations in our study was an Episcopal Church in a suburban setting. It seemed to have a specialty in family ministry, characterized by the inclusion of children in worship, many family events held in the parish to which children and parents were invited and in which they were involved, marriage enrichment seminars and weekends for couples, etc. They were the family church of that community. There were single people who also were members of the parish, but they were there by choice, or perhaps we should say "by determination." Little was offered them, and the parish did not try to provide special programming for singles. Some would say that this was a problem to be "fixed."

Surely a congregation this successful with its staff and resources could have provided ministries to singles. Yet the fact that this church has a focus, even though the focus excludes some, makes it attractive. It will need to keep a focus (or a limited number of foci) or it will not have the magnetism it now has through its clear identity. The identity of the congregation can be broadened, but within limits, in order for it not to become so diluted that it loses its appeal.

A growing Presbyterian congregation in our study found its unique ministry in outreach. It is closely associated with two other Presbyterian congregations, supporting them both financially and with volunteers; one is in a poor inner-city area, the other in a high unemployment, high crime area. In addition, they sponsor a refugee center to help refugee children became integrated into their local community, and to provide other study and recreational activities. The congregation's Appalachian Service Project is dedicated to re-painting homes of the needy in Appalachia. The congregation had a highly successful campaign to gather food and other resources (such as blankets, pillows, clothes) to give to street people. The parish has a variety of small groups made up of young adults, singles, etc., each of which picks up a special outreach ministry. Here was a congregation that lived out of and grew out of its sense of ministry as service.

A growing Unitarian Universalist congregation found its unique style in its way of providing opportunities for self-expression for its members. It prided itself on being diverse and free thinking. Its worship service was a mixture of black gospel music and a college lecture. Again, it knew who it was. This congregation knew what it was doing, and had a pretty good sense of who else would fit in and grow in this environment.

An Episcopal congregation on the Eastern seaboard found itself growing rapidly because people were attracted to the high Anglo-Catholic worship centered character of the parish.

Perhaps there is a kind of ecology of congregations wherein certain congregations attract certain people. The trick is for the church member to find the place where she or he can grow best, not for the church to attempt to meet the needs of every person who happens to walk through the door. Perhaps assimilation works best in those situations where there is enough of a match initially between the joiner and the congregation so that a mutual attraction exists (perhaps there will even be a kind of "falling in love"). But there also needs to be room to grow, to change, to be challenged. If the identification between joiner and congregation is complete at the beginning then we see self-satisfaction, insular development and in-growth rather than growth.

It should be noted that denominational loyalty among the congregations we studied was an important identity factor, but it is not as significant as it used to be especially among the Unitarians, Methodists, and Presbyterians. The exceptions were the Lutherans and Episcopalians who tended to have a higher percentage of newcomers who are of their own denomination.

How to Discover the Identity of a Congregation

One way to discover the identity of a congregation is to ask others in the community what they think is unique or special about a particular church. The responses are often surprising, insightful and fascinating. One church with which one of the authors of this book worked discovered that several in the community had dubbed the church "God's frozen chosen." That was not good news to the planning committee, but it gave them insight into who they were.

In work with congregations at the Alban Institute, we have developed an exercise that helps members ascertain the character of their identity. Usually this is done with a planning committee, but it could be carried out by any group of people interested in the life of the congregation.

Divide the group into four sub-groups and ask each to explore what it believes is the predominant quality of your congregation with regard to its category. The four categories are listed below along with clues that will help the reader get the feel for these "pieces" of identity:

1. Demographic Character

Gender	Marital Status of Members
Age	Families
Ethnicity	Singles
Geographic Area	Once Married
Education	Social class

2. Goal/Purpose/Meaning

What we are trying to accomplish?
What we are for?
What difference does our being here make?

3. Style

Open	Uptight
Laid back	Intellectual
Outgoing	Charismatic
Cautious	Workaholic
Conflict Avoiders	Conservative
Businesslike	Busy with projects
Conforming	Cold
Warm	Welcoming
High church	

4. Values

We don't talk about or share "personal" matters here
We tithe
We don't talk about money
We follow through on our promises
We are non-drinkers
We are loyal
We only allow monogamous, straight people here
We don't talk about social issues
We believe the family to be the central social unit of society
"Sinners" are welcome but they must have already repented
We don't confront deviant behavior

We usually provide the above outline to help people understand what we mean when we are describing each kind of identity. The Demographic Character of the congregation includes the naturally given attributes of the present members and those they desire to change by assimilating different kinds of members. (Be careful on this exercise, it may be that a few want to change the demographic picture and describe what they would like, not what is. If this is the

case the exercise will not elicit the current demographic picture,
but the hopes of a few.)

The Goal/Purpose/Meaning part of the congregation's identity
has to do with what it is aspiring to do and be. Here the congregation (when doing self-analysis) may focus too heavily on what the
goals *should be* and not enough on what they presently are. One
way to get a picture of the congregation's true goals is to ask how
the staff actually spend their time, to look at where the congregation's money is actually spent, and to look at what programs the
congregation supports with its participation. This will give you the
best answer to "Who are we?" Once you know who you are now,
you then have a chance of changing who you are, if that is your
aim. You can't change if you don't know where you are to begin
with.

"Style" refers to the character of the congregation, the *way* it
does things rather than *what* it does. Often congregations take on
the style of their denomination as well as developing their own pe-
culiar character.

And the values of the congregation refer to the standards it has
for how members live the Christian life. Again it will be important
to differentiate between your hoped-for standards and the ones by
which people actually abide. One way to look at this one is to notice what people actually give compared with the tithing they are
"supposed" to do.

Another method that some have used is to employ an inventory,
devised by students of congregational life, to identify theological
values or other kinds of identity in a congregation. The chapter on
"Identity" in the *Handbook for Congregational Studies*[6] describes
processes for looking at the following dimensions of a congregation's identity:

History
Heritage
World view
Symbols
Ritual
Demographics of the congregation
Character

These categories for studying a congregation's identity can provide
a fruitful way to do a careful in-depth assessment of the church's
special character.

Congregational Harmony and Cooperation

A second factor we noticed in our research on congregations which were successfully growing and assimilating new members was a high degree of good feeling among congregational members or, to put it the other way around, a low amount of conflict and disunity. There is research on church growth which shows that congregations that are bickering and in conflict tend to be less likely to grow than those in which there is good fellowship and friendliness.[7]

For there to be "good news" proclaimed in a community, somehow newcomers need to see that it is lived out in the way people relate to each other in the congregation. In the early church there was a quality of acceptance among believers which surpassed that found in other communities. In derision, and perhaps jealousy, the Romans used to say of this early church, "Look at those Christians, how they love one another."

Here is where proclamation from the pulpit needs to be translated into action within the community. Often members need help in making the translation. People are best taught to love one another in primary groups within the parish. In the 1960's we used to call this "sensitivity training." Unfortunately sensitivity training acquired a tarnished reputation back then, but even so we believe it is essential to develop opportunities for learning the skills of caring for one another and for developing greater intimacy among members; this is essential work within a congregation. Learning to love one another does not come about simply by an act of will. Usually skill training is required along with people's desire to be more loving. Leaders in the congregation who have the capacity to do this kind of skill training in the course of the ongoing life in the parish will greatly enhance the congregation's ability to deal with differences.[8] If at committee meetings the leaders take time occasionally to critique each committee's life and working style, the life of the congregation will also be greatly enhanced both in terms of its efficiency and in terms of the relationships that members have with one another. These critique periods can be the occasions for people to reflect on how loving they were to each other while doing the work of the church. Adult education courses can be offered occasionally to provide skill training for leaders. Even better are weekend retreats to do this training.

The most significant persons for enhancing congregational harmony and cooperation are the clergy. They need skills not only in preaching "good news" but also in helping people learn to be more disciplined in their caring for one another. Pastors should seek to develop these skills in in-depth leadership and conflict management training. "In-depth" means training that is long enough to help the pastor develop the skills needed (at least five days), is focused on skills (not primarily oriented to the lecture method), and is based on an accurate assessment of the pastor's current functioning.

Often the effectiveness of the pastor in helping people deal with differences is related to his or her pastoral calling and counseling. When members are uncomfortable with one another (or with the pastor) they will need opportunity to express their feelings appropriately and some help in dealing with those feelings. This frequently means that the pastor must take the initiative to make contact with those who are experiencing tension, explore the issues with them, and help them develop ways to deal with their discomfort. (These skills and actions would not be different from those used by an office manager who sees his or her working group developing unhealthy attitudes and relationships with one another.)

For clergy who are skilled at helping members identify and work through their areas of disagreement and tension, the ongoing life of a parish provides them with numerous opportunities to upgrade the quality of love and acceptance that is experienced by all people who touch the parish in any way.

The Pastor's Ability to Generate Enthusiasm

In every congregation studied the pastor was mentioned as a significant factor in "what attracted you to this parish." Over 60 percent of the time the pastor was the most frequently mentioned factor that attracted people to the congregation. The second most frequently mentioned items were connected with worship—preaching and the quality of the liturgy—which are intertwined with the style, presence and person of the pastor. When we asked people what they were looking for in a preacher they responded in this order:

1. Good sermons
2. Warmth
3. Spiritual depth

In the earliest stages of a person's relationship with a congregation a good deal of transference goes on between the newcomer and the person of the pastor (especially the head pastor or senior pastor). Somehow the person of the pastor embodies (in the imagination of the newcomer) the truth or the reality of religious experience. The newcomer hopes that somehow this pastor might be able to give him or her some help in discovering that life has order or meaning or purpose, or that it can be fulfilling and rewarding, or that one can and will know the love and acceptance of God. Early in his or her relationship with the community, the newcomer looks to the pastor more than anyone else for clues that it is possible to believe and that belief is efficacious. No matter how much the pastor might prefer not to be in this role, it is one of the most significant factors in bonding and assimilation in a congregation.

Second to the style or presence of the pastor in the chancel, newcomers will be watching how the pastor and people interact. This factor is not only important for newcomers; for most congregations it is the most important ingredient in the church life of its members. The pastor can be attractive and talented, with high energy for working with oldtimers and newcomers; yet, if there is no reciprocal response on the part of the laity, little of significance is going to happen in that parish. The reverse is also true. If you have a cadre of energetic and dedicated laypersons committed to church growth, yet have a pastor who does not cooperate or support their efforts, little of significance will happen in that congregation. Clergy are central to the life of most parishes and they can block any special effort on the part of lay people. There must also be response on the part of the laity (who can also block the pastor's special efforts) if the church is to come alive. In congregations that are alive the pastor and the people are continually turning each other on. When one or the other stops being able to turn the other on, then burnout and discouragement, even anger and resentment, overtake those who give more than they receive.

As further evidence of the importance of the pastor in helping with the assimilation process, when we asked newcomers "What almost kept you from joining the congregation?" the most frequent responses were:

1. I was ignored by the minister (The minister didn't call; I didn't think the minister knew I existed)
2. The sermons were poor
3. The service was difficult to follow.

In large churches it is probably impossible for the senior minister to greet and pay attention to all newcomers; however many newcomers still feel the need for attention from the pastor. When it is not possible for the Senior Pastor to call on all the newcomers, it is important for a minister to call even though "the" minister is not able to do this. We noted that pastoral attentiveness has less significance in the larger churches and greatest significance in congregations where less than two hundred people attend on Sunday morning.

In the churches we studied it was clergy who tended to contact newcomers first. None of the churches we observed had a lay team or individual prepared to go out and call on people after they had visited the church once or a few times. Indeed it was not lay people, most of the time, who actually invited newcomers to join the church. More often than not, if a verbal invitation was issued, it was a pastor who did the inviting. Fifty-three percent of the time no one asked the newcomer to join the church; thirty-four percent of the time a pastor asked the potential new member if he or she would like to join, and only twelve percent of the time a lay person "popped the question."

However, we did notice that it was the laity who were most important in helping the newcomer first become aware of the church. This is how people first became aware of the church:

Noticed the church while in the neighborhood	30%
A friend who is a member told me about the church	26%
A non-member in the community told me about the church	11%
A relative who is a member of the church told me about it	10%
The pastor of the church told me about it	10%
I saw an ad in the paper, phone book or other place	7%
Other (grew up here, in a group that used the building)	6%

These statistics regarding the first invitation to church seem to be similar to those of the American Church Growth Institute:

Friend or relative	79%
Pastor	6%
Sunday School	5%
Walk-in	3%
Program	3%
Special need	2%
Visitation	1%
Evangelistic Crusade	.5%

Both sets of statistics show that friends and relatives (26% + 10% = 36% in the Alban study) are the most frequent category of initial contact. And both studies show the pastor as not being a major influence on first contacts.

Looking at the key steps in the incorporation process, one can see that laity and clergy each play different but crucial roles.

Step in incorporation process	Pastor/staff	Laity
Inviting		x
Greeting		x
Follow up greeting	x	
Orienting	x	
Incorporating	?	?
Joining	x	
Sending people out	?	?

Involvement in Social Action or Social Service

In addition to these three major contextual ingredients which correlate positively with growth and assimilation, we have noted in our
studies and in some of the research on churches[9] that there is a
slight positive correlation between having social service activities in
the church and growing churches. No research shows an overwhelming positive correlation. (One Lutheran study in upstate New
York[10] even showed a slight negative correlation.) In our research
we found that most of the churches which were successfully finding
and integrating new members had some kind of outreach into the
community: they allowed other community groups to use their facilities (which brought people who would otherwise be strangers to
them into their building) and/or their members were active in
other groups, including political parties, volunteer organizations, social change groups, social groups, and self-help groups (all of which
provided opportunity for members to make contact with "outsiders"
and communicate with them about what is good about their church
experience).

Programming

Literature on growth and assimilation talks about people's need for
"places to land" when they join the church: Sunday School classes
for adults, choir, fellowship groups, sports teams, etc.[11] Schaller and
others believe that a newcomer is much more likely to "stick" if he
or she has a place to go, a place where he or she is known and
would be missed if she or he does not attend. This holds true especially in congregations larger than the family-sized congregations.
   Friendship ties seem to be the strongest bonding agent for helping members stick to a congregation. Often people join the church
looking for new friends as well as religious experience.[12] The pres-

ence of functioning small groups is about the only way that such friendship ties can easily be developed. Arlin Rothauge[13] says that one program group for every 30 to 35 active members (that means the average Sunday morning attendance) should be expected in a larger congregation. Here is another contextual factor about which the congregation can do something to help assimilate and integrate strangers into their religious home.

NOTES—CHAPTER II

1. Wade Clark Roof, et al, op. cit., p. 221.

2. There are several very fine works which will help the reader understand the identity of a congregation, three of which should be mentioned here. One is Chapter I in Lyle Schaller's book, *Assimilating New Members*, (Nashville: Abingdon 1978), entitled "What's the Glue," referring to the organizing principle or that what causes people to adhere to one another in the organization. A second is the excellent article, "Identity" in Carroll, Dudley and McKinney, *Handbook for Congregational Studies*, (Nashville: Abingdon 1986). And a third is "The Contact Boundary," the fifth chapter of *Gestalt Therapy Integrated* by Erving Polster and Miriam Polster, (New York: Vintage, 1974).

3. Dean Kelley, *Why Conservative Churches Are Growing*, (New York: Harper and Row, 1972).

4. Roof and McKinney, p. 184.

5. ibid., pp. 241-242.

6. Jackson Carroll, Carl Dudley, William McKinney (Nashville: Abingdon, 1986).

7. Roof, Hoge, Dyble and Hadaway.

8. Training for clergy and lay leaders in the local church is available from a variety of institutes and agencies in North America. The Alban Institute offers courses from its offices in various parts of the continent.

9. Roof, Hoge, Dyble and Hadaway.

10. Edward Perry, *Learning about Fishing in Upper New York*, (Syracuse: Upper New York Synod of the Lutheran Church in America, reported in ACTION INFORMATION, Sept. 1977.)

11. See especially Lyle Schaller's book, *Assimilating New Members*, (Nashville: Abingdon, 1978).

12. See Carl Dudley, *Where Have All Our People Gone*, (New York: Pilgrim Press, 1979).

13. Arlin Rothauge, *Reshaping a Congregation for a New Future*, (New York: Episcopal Church Center, 1985), p. 13.

CHAPTER III

Church Size and Assimilation

The experience of a newcomer in a tiny church will differ greatly from that of a newcomer in a medium sized church and from that of one new to a very large congregation. Arlin Rothauge, on the national staff of the Episcopal Church in Education for Mission and Ministry, has written a small book[1] that describes how the assimilation of new members into a congregation will be different depending on the size of the congregation. In order for us to appreciate those differences and their impact on the newcomer, we will explore here Rothauge's thesis regarding church size and its relation to new member assimilation.

Rothauge divides congregations into four sizes based on average Sunday morning attendance:

The Family Church	Less than 50 Average Attendance
The Pastoral Church	50-150 Average Attendance
The Program Church	150-350 Average Attendance
The Corporation Church	More than 350 Average Attendance

The Family Church

The smallest congregations are most likely to be made up of what sociologists call a cell. Carl Dudley defines a cell in this way:

> . . . members are united by common interest, beliefs, tasks and territory. They are not self-conscious about their relationships and are bound together more by sentimental ties than by contractual agreements. They have a solidarity, a feeling of belonging, nourished by experiences of intimacy and personal need.[2]

This cell is very much like a family and usually provides a social place for the members of the group which includes a kind of hier-

archy and differentiation of roles. Rothauge claims people will
emerge to fill the role of matriarch or patriarch or a "gatekeeper."
These roles may be filled in one person, or they may be shared.
The fact that these roles and their accompanying structure tend to
occur in family-sized congregations gives us some insight into what
it is like to join or be assimilated into such a church.

A couple (or one person) joining a family-sized congregation
will not find the anonymity one experiences when joining a large
social organization where there are many members and many
groups. Rothauge observes that a couple joining a family-sized congregation really is being "adopted." The church does the choosing
more than the new person does. Joining a family-sized church
might also be compared to "marrying into" a clan. Those already in
the clan spend time getting to know you; they have a lot to say
about who you are and how you will fit in. You will not be "in"
until others in the clan have had a chance to get used to you and to
assess the effect of your presence on individuals and the whole.

Newcomers in a family-sized congregation often encounter a
"gatekeeper"—the one who is cheerful and welcoming and takes
the initiative in helping the newcomer become acquainted with others in the congregation. In small congregations, however, newcomers will probably not feel a part of the group until the matriarch or
patriarch of the congregation has communicated to the newcomer
and the rest of the congregation that this new person is on the inside.

Most new pastors in very small congregations experience this
phenomenon as well. Some congregations never do let the pastor
in. People in family-sized churches assume that pastors come and
go; they are strangers in town who didn't grow up here and they
probably won't stay. Also pastors sometimes come from another social group than those in the family-sized church and have had a different educational experience (and different values about
education—and other things) than the members of that congregation. Hence, not only is it difficult for the members to open up
completely with their pastor, it is likely that the matriarch or patriarch will not give a full stamp-of-approval to this newcomer (even
though she or he is paid to be there).

People who enter family-sized congregations and stay usually
have other family or friendship ties to someone in the congregation. Those who don't have these ties usually don't have the for-
bearance and persistence to hang around long enough finally to be
adopted. For most, true adoption into the family-sized congregation
is a long-term process.

The Pastoral Church

The pastoral-sized church has between 50 and 150 people on Sunday morning.[3] In this size parish there may be two or three cells in the congregation, each of which functions like a clan. Often these primary groups are indeed extended family units, but in some pastoral sized congregations the cells unite around a common interest such as music or a Sunday school class or the women's organization. A leadership circle replaces the patriarch/matriarch and quite often the pastor is at the center of this circle.

These congregations are often structured like a wheel rather than a pyramid. At the hub is the minister with the spokes being the various cells that are in touch with and work with each other. In a congregation of this size the pastor is usually, quite literally, involved in everything. The pastor attends all the church meetings, goes to all public gatherings and does most of the ministering. If people need to be called on, the pastor does it; if a couple need instruction on how to conduct and carry out a wedding and reception at the church, the pastor does it, if newcomers show up, the pastor calls on them. This is expected not only by the pastor, but by the members, *and by the newcomers.*

Those coming into a pastoral-sized congregation will expect attention from the clergyperson; they will most likely bond first with him or her and later on with others in the church. This can cause a problem, because the pastor cannot continue to give attention to those who are "in," but must work on bringing others in as well. In this size church, therefore, there may be problems with assimilation and recruitment because the pastor is limited in the number of newcomers he or she can bring in at a time. Many pastors who have served this size church say that members tend to be casual, even uninterested, in the newcomers, and that it is up to the pastor to get them interested.

Membership seems to be granted much more easily in the pastoral-sized church than in the family-sized church. But inclusion into the core circle may prove difficult and may take a significant amount of time.

The Program Church

The program sized congregation has between 150 and 350 people in church on an average Sunday. In this size congregation, the pastor cannot attend to all of the organization or all of the people; it is too large and there are too many. The congregation seems to pull itself into a more democratic organization than in the smaller churches. That is, members (and boards and committees) depend more on representatives to get the various tasks of maintenance and ministry done in the church. More work is delegated by the pastor to lay people and committees, and the governing board finds itself unable to "stay on top of" everything. It finds itself dependent on the work of others and the reporting of others.

In the program-sized church the pastor spends less time in direct contact with members, and especially with newcomers. To maintain the institution, the pastor must spend many more hours training, supervising and coordinating the work of others. Sometimes congregations that are growing from a pastoral-sized church to a program-sized church become annoyed with their pastor who seems to be less interested in newcomers (and for that matter shut-ins and those who are hospitalized). It may not be the case that the pastor is less interested, but rather that the pastor is overwhelmed by the pressing needs of coordination and management that cannot be avoided. Newcomers and shut-ins may make fewer immediate and visible demands than the staff, boards, buildings, funerals, and people coming in by appointment for counseling and weddings.

Congregational life in the program-sized church may have less unity than the family or pastoral-sized churches. There may be several centers of life or energy around which different members gather. In the pastoral-sized church the members join the whole—they join the church. In the program-sized church, members are more likely to join a part of the church—a church school class, a choir, a couple's group, a study group, a group involved in outreach.

Thus, entry and assimilation occurs in a subgroup, rather than in the whole. The assimilators (those who are helping the newcomer enter the congregation) are really helping people join smaller groups in the church rather than helping them join the whole church. The program-sized (or larger) congregation exploring its entry processes will want to look at how people can be helped to be assimilated into the smaller parts of the larger system, rather than into the whole.

Newcomers in the program-sized congregation may experience several entry and assimilation experiences. Perhaps their first experience was being assimilated into a short-term new members' or inquirers' class. After getting acquainted with a few people there, they were officially welcomed into the church. The newcomers then had to find (if they had not already found) other "places to land." Sometimes this place was a church school class or other small group in the church. If the newcomers have been recognized for their leadership potential in the new member's class or church school class, they may be nominated for or invited to work on a church committee. Again, an assimilation process will be necessary because the new person will not know and will not be known by most of the workers on the committee.

One can see how easy it would be for the newcomer to get lost in a complex system. Unless the newcomer feels motivated to want to be an insider, she or he may easily stray from further participation.

The Corporation Church

In the very largest churches, with more than 350 in attendance on Sunday morning, one finds an even more complex and diverse array of programs, ministries, classes and committees. The Senior Pastor seems even more distant from most members than in a smaller organization. The preaching, the building, the size of the organization, the credentials of the leaders, the reputation of the church all instill respect and reverence and may cause the new person to be reticent about moving easily into the church.

Frequently in a church of this size ministers or leaders of departments function toward newcomers much like pastors in pastoral-sized churches. The newcomer may join a department and get acquainted and assimilated there, much as he or she would in the program-sized church. The senior pastor is known by relatively few people in the church; she or he functions as a symbol of unity and stability in an otherwise complex and seemingly fragmented organization.

Church Size and Assimilation

So why have we included this discussion of church sizes in this book on assimilation? We have noted in some congregations that members who have had good experience in a congregation of one size go to another and try to replicate that experience in a church where that kind of assimilation process won't work. It is obvious to members of small, single cell congregations that what works for big, old First Church Downtown doesn't fit their situation, and they will easily tell that to you, their pastor and anyone else who cares to listen. However, it may be much more difficult for the pastor coming from the pastoral sized church to understand or respond to the different demands placed on his or her time in program-sized churches, both by the situation and by the members who may be proposing programs and activities out of their pastoral- or family-sized previous experience.

Further, if you want to develop a formal assimilation process in your church (that is, one which is planned and implemented in an intentional way), then you will want to design a system that fits the peculiarities of the dynamics of a smaller or larger congregation. You need to plan ways to overcome some of the drawbacks of your size congregation and to build on its strengths. For example, in a pastoral-sized church the members may do better to plan to work with the pastor in helping new members get acquainted with the congregation rather than trying to do this without the pastor's involvement. Larger congregations will have more resources to develop "places to land" for newcomers and can set themselves to the tasks of developing processes to help the stranger find an appropriate place where he or she can get acquainted and grow.

NOTES—CHAPTER III

1. Arlin J. Rothauge, *Sizing Up a Congregation: for New Member Ministry*, (Seabury Professional Services).

2. Carl Dudley, *Making the Small Church Effective*, (Nashville: Abingdon, 1978, p. 32).

3. Don't take these numbers too literally. There are some congregations that have the numbers to exhibit the characteristics of a pastoral-size congregation but act like a family-size church. This is sometimes a problem in growing churches where they have trouble stretching to new ways of functioning under the altered demands of the larger system. Shrinking congregations also find themselves organized as a program church and attempting to function as a program church, but have lost so many members that the structure for the large institution no longer fits their diminished proportions.

CHAPTER IV

Attracting and Recruiting New Members

When we first showed the manuscript of this book to several readers this chapter perplexed them. "I thought," queried one reader, "you said in the second chapter that the successful congregations you studied, for the most part, had no formal recruiting or assimilating systems. How come you're now listing a whole bunch of stuff that seems like what you would read in any 'let's clean up our act' book?" True enough, we reply to that reader and others who may be asking the same question, the most powerful attracting features of a local congregation are not the items we will list in this chapter. We talk about visibility here. But two of the churches in our study were so hidden and tucked away that the first question asked by newcomers at this church was almost always "How did you find this place the first time you came?" And the first question asked by the old-timers of the newcomer was "Did you have trouble finding us?" What is described in this chapter is not guaranteed, sure fire, "this'll get'em every time" salesmanship. Rather it is a description of some incorporation procedures that also help.

If we learned one thing in our research it was that the essence of attracting and the essence of recruiting lies in having something to offer. If the church has something to give people, they will beat their way in. They are attracted by the power of the message lived and proclaimed within that "place." If the church does not have a special identity, an enthusiastic heart, a healing elixir, whatever is done to increase the visibility, to advertise, to recruit will mean little because, even if the church does get a few "prospects," they will be just that. That is, like the word "prospect," which connotes a lackadaisical hope more than it does commitment, these "nibblers" will approach the church with their bellies full and perhaps "nose" the bait. They will not be like those who are hungry and out seriously looking for something of substance, and when they sense that they have found it will rush for the bait, wriggling their way into a place where they think they can get what they want.

Focussing on the items in this chapter can also be a way of not dealing with the central issues: what it really takes to be an attractive congregation that is discovered by people who then assimilate themselves. For that's the way most successfully growing congregations work. The church doesn't assimilate people. They assimilate themselves. Actually, it's a little annoying to have to put up with strangers all the time hanging around wanting to learn the lore, wanting to get what the others have got there, wanting to give advice, wanting to be wanted. And church people know that. That may be why we never really set up effective recruiting and assimilating systems. We just might be successful! But we digress—the point is that the leadership of a congregation can get itself caught up in fixing the building, training people to call on friends or strangers, getting themselves involved in community groups, opening their building to the public, and setting up signs on their lawn perpendicular to the highway. They can get so busy with these activities that they won't have to address the questions: Why are we here? What is God calling us to do? How can we be effective?

So let's not let this chapter get in our way. Those of us who are about the Lord's work know that we are, and we are going to get on with it. We can be helped in that task by developing systems, programs, processes that will assist those who really want to find us and join us. That is what this chapter is about. It will be helpful to those who know what they are about. It will not be helpful to those who don't know who they are or what they are there for, but just want to have a nice church.

We will now focus on two aspects of how members discover and/or get invited into a congregation at the very beginning of their acquaintance with it. *Recruiting* will refer to the active reaching out of members or staff to people who are not familiar with or are just becoming familiar with the congregation. *Attracting* will refer to what is done to make the congregation's presence known, but does not involve members actively contacting or interacting with those who do not know this congregation.

Attracting

In Chapter II we included a table that showed how people first became aware of the church they joined. At that point we presented the table to illustrate the relative importance of the pastor in the joining process. Let us look at it again to see which factors seem most important in attracting newcomers:

Noticed the building in neighborhood	30%
Friend told me about it	26%
Other (Pastor, grew up here, group such as scouts, school in church)	15%
Non-member in the community told me	11%
Family member brought me	10%
Saw an advertisement	7%

The first thing that one notices in these statistics is that only 37%, a little more than a third of the people, had no previous experience with their congregation before they showed up. Either they grew up there, they were in a group ancillary to the church or someone told them about it—a friend (26%), a family member (10%), or a non-member (11%) Note that these were churches in a metropolitan area! Now none of these churches had an evangelism committee. None had a paid staff person who called on people or a volunteer who took it upon himself or herself to "go after" people in the community. Something was happening in these churches that made the members (and non-members) feel good about sharing what was happening there and communicating that feeling of enthusiasm to others. One cannot deny that visibility of the building and advertising are important, but these factors do not have the same weight as the attraction that comes from the testimony of "satisfied customers."

Let us briefly review some of the things churches do to increase their visibility.

Physical Presence in the Neighborhood

Visibility

The physical presence of the church in the neighborhood has been noted by many students of church growth and development as an important factor in "inviting" people to the church. If the church is not visible, fewer in the community will know that the church is there. Churches that are built on *cul de sacs*, in-out-of-the-way, low-traffic areas; churches that are hidden from view in high-traffic areas, or are not distinguishable as a church will also be disadvantaged in attracting those who may choose their church because they notice it in the neighborhood.

Condition of Property

The church must be seen to attract those who are drawn by a building, and its condition will have an effect on whether this type of stranger will come to explore further. Each of the choices the church planner makes in this regard will alienate some and attract others, such as whether the building is a white New England meeting house, stone gothic, or a "wee chapel in the pines." Those designing the church should pay more attention to whether the architecture reflects the theology, identity, and tradition of the congregation than on whether it will be aesthetically pleasing to the greatest number. The state of a facility's upkeep and maintenance determines its attractiveness in important ways. Deteriorating, unkempt and unsafe buildings are significant "turn-offs" to those unfamiliar with the warm and loving people inside.

The condition of the property is not only a significant factor for those who pass by, but also for those who enter the facility. What happens to a young couple with an infant, out church hunting, who enter a congregation on a Sunday morning to worship will have a significant impact on whether they return. If there is no place for them to leave their child, if there is a place and it is not spotless, if the care provided seems haphazard or inattentive, if different people staff the nursery each Sunday, or if the facility is overcrowded and insufficiently staffed, the church will be perceived as an uninviting place to be a regular participant. Each part of the building should be evaluated for its possibilities of "turning-off" visitors who don't know this church, especially the condition of the rest rooms, the kitchen and church school rooms (which sometimes communicate to the stranger that what goes on in them is insignificant, perhaps lackadaisical).

Accessibility

Accessibility is another key to attracting total strangers. Of course, making the church accessible to handicapped people will make it more inviting to such persons. But accessibility is also an issue for the able-bodied. Churches that hide or block their entrances with locks, peepholes, and speaker phones will seem less attractive to those who don't know what is going on inside. (Of course, some churches have no choice but to resort to protective devices for the safety of the property and those within the building; however, the cost in attractiveness will be notable.)

Sometimes access seems easy to the insider, but is not easy to the outsider. Those who have been around for years may know why the main (visible from the street) doors are locked—perhaps almost no one comes in that way, because most members drive and come in the back way from the parking lot. Yet the stranger who finds the main doors locked may be embarrassed by his or her inability to get in on the first try, which calls attention to his or her status as one who is "on the outs."

Advertising

Signs

Signs provide another help to those who have never been to your church. Signs in the neighborhood can direct newcomers from a busy street and let them know you exist. Signs at the building entrance and in the building let people know where to go for what: the main office, the pastor's study, church school, coffee hour, bathrooms. Greeters who wear signs such as these also help people who don't know what this place is about: "New today? Ask me," or "Greeter," or "My name is _____. May I assist you?"

But more important is a sign outside the church that lets visitors know about who you are. The following advice about church signs is taken from Steve Dunkin's helpful book *Church Advertising:*[1]

1. A sign parallel to the road is fine for pedestrians and is probably more aesthetically pleasing, but it is impossible for car riders to read. *Put up a sign that is at right angles to the road* and which can be read from a car traveling at the speed limit in either direction.
2. *Make it big enough* to be read easily. On a street with a 60 kph (40 mph) speed limit, a 4 x 8 foot sign would be about right. Place it as close to the road as city ordinances permit.
3. *Aim at legibility.* That means using very plain and easily read block letters. Avoid fancy lettering and never, never, never use an "Olde English" script. It is difficult to read, and besides, it gives the church an archaic air. That is not the kind of image you want to project.
4. *Keep your sign simple.* The most effective probably are those made of 4 x 8 sheets of plywood in a 4 x 4 inch cedar frame. It is doubtful that the sign made of brick or angel stone, surrounded by shrubs, and with a changeable print board enclosed in glass, is worth the expense.
5. Along with a listing of the times of worship and church school, *include a phrase or slogan* describing an essential characteristic of the congregation:
   Country-style Friendliness in the City
   A Warm Fellowship with People Like You

Print Media

The Yellow Pages, newspaper ads, newspaper features, parish brochures, and community newsletters are common ways churches get out the word about where they are and what they are doing. Parish brochures are probably more helpful as an orientation guide to people who come to the church, though some congregations that are just starting have been successful in attracting small numbers of people through mass mailings to particular neighborhoods with carefully designed brochures.

Community newsletters can be helpful in generating goodwill and better visibility in the neighborhood where the church is located. These are usually one- or two-page documents which focus primarily on news of community interest with prominent inclusion of the church's name, logo, activities, services, and times of worship (though these are not purported to be the central message of the newsletter).

Radio and Television

Radio and television can be useful as a way to get the word out about the presence of your congregation, though they are quite expensive. To give an example of the use of an integrated advertising campaign, the Reformed Church in America, as a part of a church-wide church growth effort, decided to move four new congregations into the northern parts of Dallas. Five clergy were hired: an executive minister, who was to leave when the four congregations were up and running, and four pastors who were to stay as ministers of the congregations. The denomination rented a nice office in a central shopping mall where the five clergy began their work.

To acquaint Dallas with the fact that the Reformed Church was coming to town and who they were historically and theologically, the project began advertising on radio and television.

This advertising was followed up by bus loads of volunteers who came to Dallas from Iowa and Michigan to randomly phone all the households in the areas where the four new congregations were to be located. The callers asked if the people had seen the ads and if they would be interested in a visit from the pastor who was starting the church near them. Of course, the callers were turned down nine times out of ten. If they had been doing this alone or had been doing it for more than a week at a time, the caller burn-out rate would have been phenomenal. However, about the time the job would have become terribly frustrating, the volunteer callers went back to their homes and churches in Iowa and Michigan and a fresh load of callers arrived in Dallas.

When the callers got an affirmative response to their request for a minister to visit, that pastor would make a call in the home at an appointed time. Of course, the pastors were turned down many, many times, but their turndown rate was much less than that of the phone callers, and within a couple of years four self-sustaining congregations with ministries, buildings and programs were up and running. This is a process which incorporates both the attracting and the recruiting of members, and it illustrates how advertising can be effectively used to help with church growth.

Concerned Presence in the Community

Almost all of the churches observed in our research had developed ways to serve people who were not members of their congregation.[2] These efforts will acquaint people with your congregation, though the numbers of newcomers that are likely to come as a result will be very small. (The chart on page 39 shows only 15 percent of the people joining the church come because of activities held at the church, as well as other factors *including acquaintance with the pastor and previous participation in the congregation!*)

Participation by Members in Community Affairs

One way new people become familiar with a church is by meeting members who are working in community groups. Some churches ask their members to serve on community boards and committees, such as coordinating councils, family planning agencies, health care centers, coops, and so on as representatives of the congregation. This is a way of increasing visibility, but, in our opinion, if such participation is undertaken for these reasons it is shallow and self-serving. Increased visibility is a by-product of participation in community affairs, not a motive for it.

Participation by Groups or the Whole Church in Community Affairs

Other congregations (such as All Saints Church in Pasadena, California, with its Creative Communications Council) have groups who do research on community matters and acquaint those who can do something about them with the needs of the area. Some churches have established a group within the church to meet a need in the community, such as the development of a family planning clinic by Trinity Episcopal Church in Muscatine, Iowa.

Some churches rent a booth to sell food or handcrafts at community art fairs with their name, brochures and publicity material prominently displayed.

Availability of Building for Use by Other Groups in the Community

Most mainline churches, of course, allow their buildings to be used by others in the community—which is a good way to provide a service to one's neighbors, and to acquaint outsiders with the location, mission, or kinds of people in the church. Bringing people into the building makes it possible for them to see your bulletin boards, peruse your book rack, explore your other programs (if they are prominently and attractively displayed), and "bump into" members who may be involved in other activities. "Outsiders" may use local church facilities to attend Weight Watchers meetings, aerobic dance classes, Scout troops, or Alcoholics Anonymous. They may come to vote, to attend community councils or to attend a peace protest.

Recruiting

Recruiting new members (or what many churches call evangelism—though recruiting is not what the New Testament means by "evangelism") can be an effective way to add members to a church. New congregations do it or die. Most of them would not exist if it were not for aggressive pastors and members who pushed themselves on strangers and successfully dragged, motivated or enticed folks into their new venture.

However, few new congregations sustain the early zeal to recruit and, after the church has grown to a place where it can financially sustain itself, recruiting efforts usually flag. The most recent statistics of which we are aware on how people are brought into the church were published by Elmer Towns in his article "Evangelism: The How and Why."[3] He gives figures very similar to those seen elsewhere:

How People are Brought into the Church

By Advertisement	2%
By the Pastor	6%
By Organized Evangelistic Outreach	6%
By Friends and Relatives	86%

We believe that the reason these first three figures are so low is that members of established churches are not comfortable with and will not participate in "organized evangelistic outreach," for the most part. (Certainly none of the successful churches in our sample did.) Other research doesn't show recruiting faring much better. In their studies of churches that were growing, Roof, Hoge, *et al*[4] showed a slight positive correlation between church growth and the presence of a group working at recruiting new members. However, other research does not support this. Edward Perry did an informal study of declining congregations in the Upper New York Synod of the Lutheran Church in America and reported[5]:

In the 26 case studies, when we paired congregations in similar social settings and by similar size, those with evangelism committees tended to report lower accessions and less growth than those without committees. This result really "blew our minds!" It especially blew mine when I recalled the strong observation of McGavran and Arn in *How to Grow a Church* that no congregation grows without a solid core of lay leaders who are willing, capable, and actually engaging in outreach.

Perry's findings may be more the result of the fact that churches having trouble with growth are those which are most likely to set up evangelism committees. *And* it may be the case that setting up such a committee is foreign to the culture of the congregation and, therefore, not an effective tool for recruitment and growth. Nonetheless, we believe that the readers of this book should take seriously the problems inherent in attempting to "set up" a committee or individual to do recruiting of strangers to the church. Much more "pay off" is likely to come from more informal processes that function less like indoctrination and more like contagion: involvement in this church is a communicable experience caught by proximity and contact rather than inculcation, indoctrination, or inoculation.

Informal Invitations by Members of Friends and Family

In most of the research done on church growth, McGavran's included[6], by far the largest number of people who join the church come through contacts by members with their friends and family.

The way the church growth movement deals with this understanding that most new participation in churches comes through the contacts of members with friends or families is to set up systems to recruit new people to the church. We have had little experience with such methods, frankly, and none of the growing churches in our research group had such committees. Those in the church growth movement suggest a process like that described with enthusiasm by George Hunter in his article "The Bridges of Contagious Evangelism."[7] He writes:

A Mennonite church in Japan employs the following strategy: During the three-month, one-night-per-week, one-on-one post conversion training for new members, the trainer and convert develop a list of all the person's names in the new convert's active social network. The trainer, near the end of the three months, asks the convert to underline all the names of persons thought not to be active disciples through any congregation. The trainer asks, "Which of these (underlined) people do you have some influence with?" Those names are circled, and the trainer and convert together reach out to each of those persons. As some of those persons are attracted into discipleship, the strategy is repeated. Most churches could develop and execute a similar strategy, appropriately adapted to their culture and situation.

In a church growth manual developed for congregations bent on *Finding the Way Forward*, I offer to church leaders a simple set of strategic guidelines that have helped other congregations:

1. Secure the names of all undiscipled persons within the social webs of your active credible Christians. Have some member of your evangelism committee visit, with each active member, the undiscipled persons he or she has listed.

2. As you win some of those target persons, secure the names of their undiscipled relatives and friends. Have an evangelism committee member visit, with the new believer, these people to be reached.

3. Survey each member each season to get the names of new undiscipled prospects. This will continually reveal a fertile harvest field for your church—undiscipled persons who are already linked to one or more persons in your congregation.

4. As you reach out, do not in every case attempt to gather Christ's prepared harvest in just one visit or conversation. Be prepared to visit with persons a half-dozen more times to help them work through what their response to the invitation might be.

5. As some of your people begin serving as new bridges for others, reinforce this action through appropriate public recognition. For instance when you receive new members into the church, invite members who served as bridges for them to stand with them, and pray both for new disciples and their human bridges.

These methods would appear overly bold and crass to members of the congregations we studied. They have the key ingredients of a recruitment program based on a "marketer's" knowledge of what gets results:

Training of members in how to identify potential recruits (that is, friends and relatives)

Training of members in how to approach potential recruits and sustain meaningful conversations about becoming acquainted with the gospel and the church

Supervision and support of the members who are doing the recruiting

Recognition of the members who have been effective in bringing new participants

The problem with a system set up in just this way in a so-called mainline church is that this kind of a recruiting program does not respect an important norm of the religious culture of moderate and liberal congregations, which is that religion—and especially your own religious experience—is not something you speak of aloud or boldly.

In our research, when we asked newcomers if the congregation offered to train them to recruit other potential members, 89 percent said "no" and 11 percent said "yes." In only one of the 14 congregations in the Philadelphia/Atlanta portion of our study did more newcomers answer "yes" to this question than answered "no;" it happened to be a Lutheran church which responded 16 "yes," 13 "no." One Presbyterian congregation came close with 7 "yes," and 13 "no" answers.

From past Alban Institute research we know that it is not easy for people to talk about spiritual and religious matters within their congregational community. Jean Haldane has done some excellent research that describes this reality. In her monograph she describes how reticent laity are to talk about the religious pilgrimage:

The personal journey *is* personal, not shared with many (not even those close), surprisingly private. Few want to make it public for fear of appearing, as one person said, "a freak in a non-religious world." These people interviewed are *not* dying to bare their souls in small groups; that gets all mixed up with the thought of emotionalism and witnessing or arguing about doctrine—and none want that.

The private nature of the journey is partly responsible for the fact that it appears to "occur on the side" in the church. It is not talked about there. There is a veritable "conspiracy of silence" about it. It is peripheral to, not parallel with the church. It is simply there, untapped and unrecognized, an underground of experience that is the personal context for what happens to each person at church. Another fact that discourages people from talking about the religious journey is that no one in the church

ever asks about their personal faith and practice. Several spoke
of fear of judgement and not measuring up to some standard
images of a church-goer or Episcopalian.[8]

This reticence to talk about religious experience becomes (in moderate and liberal churches) a conspiracy of silence which is a part
of the organizational norms of the mainline church. "We don't talk
about those things here." The pastor may talk about them. They may
be discussed with the pastor in a counseling session, but not cas-
ually with other members in groups or individually. So the norms
are such that members protect one another from the necessity of
talking about personal religion. If a member of the church, then,
started talking with another person about his or her spiritual
growth, it would cause each significant discomfort.

What does this say about recruiting programs in moderate to liberal churches? Based on the experience of the successful congregations we studied and our own experience with numerous other
congregations, we believe that an all-out, frontal approach to recruiting members will generate more resistance than it will be
worth in terms of effectiveness. The congregation's growth will be
better served if the members are gently and regularly made aware
that "evangelism" happens best among those we know and care for
and that the greatest possibilities for growth will be among those
who are already known to the church members. However, the most
effective evangelism will come from unplanned, spontaneous enthusiasm members share (perhaps not even consciously) with friends
and relatives. The church will do better to focus on developing its
own ministry, on serving others, on attending to the Lord's work
and let this serve as an attractor of newcomers rather than "beating
the bushes," which is more likely to drive out and frighten than to
attract and draw in. Those drawn in will be drawn to the promise of
meaning and support, to a community where they are wanted for
who they are and not just for what they can provide.

Invitations upon Inquiries about Weddings and Baptisms

Another opportunity for recruiting arises in the context of inquiries
from non-members about a wedding or baptism. Some congregations have rules that only those who are active in the congregation
may avail themselves of these rites. Churches open to outsiders for
these rites will naturally be able to share more about the church
and the opportunities for growth and service it affords.

Re-inviting Drop Outs

This is a popular "quick cure" often suggested by church members. Alice Mann says in her very fine book on incorporating new members:[9]

> When a parish begins to look at its responsibility to reach out and invite the unchurched into relationship with Christ and his Church, someone will almost invariably say, "We shouldn't begin to spend our energy on looking for new members until we have brought back our own inactive members." Such a comment often strikes a chord in lay leaders. A parish which adopts this approach has come to a dead end before it begins, for both theological and practical reasons.
>
> Theologically, we are not at liberty to set "priorities" among the essential elements of the Baptismal Covenant, to decide that loving the neighbor within a parish is more important than loving the neighbor who has not met Christ and his Church. Because so many Episcopal parishes have avoided even mentioning the word "evangelization" for so many years, one suspects that the diversion of attention to internal pastoral care is a flight from what *appears* to be the more difficult and challenging task.
>
> Practically speaking, the parish's pastoral ministry to its "disaffected" members is one of the most difficult and demanding of ministries, and one from which we can expect little numerical success. (One does it anyway, because we are called to love one another.) John Savage's study *The Bored and Apathetic Church Member* raises up two important facts we have to face. One, it is crucial to follow up on someone who has "dropped out" (behaviorally) *within three months* of their disappearance from the scene. Even if they were not in a hostile state when they drifted away, they are likely to become increasingly alienated as they conclude that no one cares that they are gone. Second, those who have settled into a hurt and angry state, and have been in that state for some times, are very unlikely to return, even with good pastoral intervention.

Summary

This chapter has not taken the usual approach to church "evangelism," suggesting that everybody work harder at attracting and drawing in members as the way to build your church. We just don't see evidence that people will do this kind of work in mainline congregations, *unless they are new church starts.* At the core of attracting and assimilating others to the church, and to the Gospel, is the health of the church as a community of believers and commitment on the part of those believers to serving the Lord.

This does not mean that the institution turns its back on recruiting and attracting, rather it means that the church should primarily attend to its main business of worship, education, and service and put further down the list of its priorities various kinds of marketing and salesmanship.

NOTES—CHAPTER IV

1. Steve Dunkin, *Church Advertising: A Practical Guide*, (Nashville: Abingdon, 1982, pp. 104-105).

2. The data on the effectiveness for church growth regarding involvement of members in the community and use of the building by "outside" groups is mixed. Roof, Hoge, Dyble and Hadaway (op. cit., p. 216) have this to say: ". . .organizing the disadvantaged and financial support for activities customarily associated with churches—Scouts, rehabilitation for example—are positively related with membership growth; but the use of congregational facilities by groups concerned with social action and explicit efforts at changing society tend to be inversely related."

3. Elmer Towns, "Evangelism: The How and Why," in *Church Growth: State of the Art*, C. Peter Wagner, Editor, (Wheaton: Tyndale, 1986, pp. 43-55).

4. Op. cit.

5. Edward Perry, "Where Are the People?", ACTION INFORMATION, (Washington, The Alban Institute, Inc., Sept. 1977).

6. Donald A. McGavran is one of the most assertive proponents of church growth by aggressive "evangelism." He is the founder of the School of World Mission and Institute of Church Growth at Fuller Seminary in Pasadena, and is known as the "founder of the church growth movement."

7. This article is in Wagner, ed., *Church Growth: The State of the Art*, op. cit., pp. 74-75.

8. Jean Haldane, *Religious Pilgrimage*, (Washington: The Alban Institute, Inc., 1975, pp. 10-11). (Out of print, but available to members as an On Demand Publication.)

9. Alice B. Mann, *Incorporation of New Members in the Episcopal Church: A Manual for Clergy and Lay Leaders*, (Philadelphia: Ascension, 1983, p. 35). Also see Robert T. Gribbon, *When People Seek the Church*, (Washington: The Alban Institute, Inc.) for a further discussion of these points.

CHAPTER V

Incorporating

Once the new arrivals have decided to "drop in" on church one Sunday, they move into another stage of involvement. This stage seems to include two distinct phases which occur before new persons actually join the church (either behaviorally or through a joining ceremony or both). These two phases of incorporation we call testing and affiliating.

Testing

It is not easy to walk into a strange church. At some point that third of the newcomers who drop in because they saw the building or some kind of advertising go beyond looking around and risk visiting a church. Even those who have heard about the place and have been invited are likely to be apprehensive or nervously excited the first time they cross the threshold. What happens to them during this initial visit is crucial to whether they will come back because they are quite likely to be tentative and non-commital toward both the members and programs offered of the church. But to be frank, not only are they checking us out, the members are checking them out as well. If something doesn't sit right for the already existing members, the newcomer may get even less attention than would otherwise be the case.

Being Recognized as a Visitor

The assimilation process functions smoothest when the stranger is recognized as needing to be helped into the congregation. One does not feel welcomed if he or she is left alone, unattended, feeling lost and helpless. It will not surprise the reader by now to learn that our successful churches got mixed reviews with regard to recognizing the fact that they had a new person in their midst.

58% of the newcomers in these churches said they were singled out or identified as a newcomer.

42% claimed they were not.

Again, we see that even in churches that are successful at assimilating new people often the most rudimentary courtesies were missed. The newcomers who were not recognized felt slightly distanced from the congregation in not having their presence acknowledged in some way.

In reflecting on the entry experience of the people in the churches in our study and on what other congregations we know have done, we believe that there is no "right way" to recognize a person or couple on their first visit. So. much depends upon the visitors. Those tending towards "extraversion" will appreciate being identified openly as newcomers with a flower pinned on them or a special name tag, or being asked to stand up and identify themselves at the time of parish announcements etc. Those tending toward "introversion" may feel just the opposite. The last thing introverts want is someone making a big fuss over them on their initial visit. Their preference is to slip in and out of the worship so they can reflect on the experience in privacy elsewhere. Greeters who are sensitive to this can tell the difference. In either case, we believe it is considerate to the stranger to help her find her way and useful to the church to get her name and address. No follow up work is possible without this bit of information. Even those tending towards introversion will not mind being quietly asked to sign the guest register before leaving the church.

To help the person who has never been to this church before and to make follow-up possible, it is a good idea to alert appropriate people to the presence of the newcomer. If there are children present, someone from the Sunday Church School could offer an invitation to an appropriate class. Depending upon the size of the congregation, an informal introduction to the pastor is often helpful. Indeed, the pastor's reaction to the newcomer is often perceived by the newcomer as the single most important contact on an early visit (which we will discuss further below), and may tip the balance toward moving toward or away from affiliation with this congregation. Where possible we recommend introducing the newcomer to a person or family who seem to match most closely the visitor's age, level of education, occupation, etc. We believe that these kinds of connections help the stranger to feel more at home and more identified with the church and its members. If the new person identifies with the people in the church, he or she is more likely to return.

A Washington, DC, Episcopal parish put the following notices in the Sunday bulletin to encourage members and visitors to overcome their mutual bashfulness:

> *Notice to Visitors.* People who attend St. Mark's regularly are for the most part kind and friendly people, but they tend to be a bit shy and self-conscious with strangers. They are afraid of greeting people they think are new and discovering that "the visitors" have been attending St. Mark's for years. So please help. Identify yourself to the people nearest you and ask them to tell you about our church.
>
> *Notice to St. Mark's Members.* Please do your best to make everyone feel welcome. Always introduce yourself to the people sitting near you if you don't know their names. In order to avoid the embarrassment of mistaking a long time member for a visitor, use the following ploy: "Good morning. My name is _____. I've been coming to St. Mark's for _____ (years/weeks). How about you?"

Facilitating visitors' participation in the worship liturgy also helps make them more comfortable on their first visit. When visitors appear to be lost somewhere between the Sunday bulletin, the hymnal and the prayer book, an old timer's quiet and unobtrusive guidance can be a kind and welcome gesture. Greeters or church ushers who can tell the difference between first-time visitors and oldtimers can facilitate this by seating newcomers beside others who can quietly guide them through the worship service. (Greeters who stand at the door with a corsage and a handshake are not likely to be as helpful for assimilation purposes as a person who can walk with, ask questions of, and guide the new arrival. Perhaps congregations should consider having both formal greeters and more mobile and active welcomers.)

Expectations

Everyone visiting a church for the first time carries an image of what a "church ought to be like." Rarely are their expectations met in full. Yet when some of their expectations are met—or when they experience some pleasant surprises—newcomers are more likely to return for a second visit. For this reason we believe it is important to ask (perhaps not on the first visit), "What are you looking for in a church family?" Only seventeen percent of the people in our study said they were asked this question as newcomers. Eighty-three percent said they were not asked this question by the church they joined.

The person helping the newcomer become acquainted with the congregation needs an answer to this question in order to help him or her determine whether the church is a good "fit." The task here is not to trick the new person into believing that your church has what he or she needs—that may lead to disappointment and, perhaps, trouble both for the newcomer and the church. Rather, the task is to help both the church and the outsider discover whether they will be good for each other.

Frequently it is not entirely clear to the newcomer what he or she is looking for, and sometimes it is not appropriate to ask. When we asked the newcomers in our sample of congregations what they were looking for in a church, the following three items were most prominent:

1. Warmth, welcome, caring community
2. Meaningful worship/sermons
3. A family place for children.

If the person greeting and introducing the new person to the church does not know specifically what it is that this individual is looking for in a church the above "needs" could be assumed until the greeter and stranger get better acquainted. As this welcomer discovers the new person's needs and interests, he or she will be able to direct the newcomers to appropriate individuals and groups to help with the journey toward affiliation. What is important here is that someone pay attention to the new person. Newcomers will be able to discover whether a church is the place for them only if someone in the congregation spends time with them.

Affiliating

The stage between the first visit to the parish and finally joining we call "affiliating." It may last from one month to two years. When we asked newcomers when they felt accepted in their new congregation, 42 percent said, "immediately upon the first visit." It re-emphasized for us the importance of that first visit during which the momentum to join begins for some people. They continued to expect good things from their new congregation, and those good things seemed to materialize.

With others it takes longer. Beyond the first visit, no special period stands out. We asked those who had just joined:

"When did you feel accepted in this congregation?"

42%   Immediately upon first visit
10%   Within one month
 6%   Within three months
 5%   Within six months
 9%   Within one year
10%   When I joined
 7%   I still don't feel totally accepted
 3%   During a class

A similar response occurred when we asked:

"How long did you attend before joining?"

26%   one to three months
36%   three to twelve months
12%   twelve months
18%   more than twelve months
 4%   have not joined

The "affiliating" stage is like courtship. The parish is still trying to put on its best face, and the newcomers are working at leaving a good impression with clergy, leaders and members. This stage is usually characterized by regular church and Sunday school attendance. The newcomers have ceased to "shop around" for a congregation and have settled into this one for a deeper try. This stage is highlighted by

—feeling accepted and liked by people important to them
—satisfaction with the Sunday School their children attend
—clergy who are seen as "good enough" or even superior.

The decision to return is influenced by many factors. Perhaps something of what the newcomers were looking for was discovered—but certainly not everything. Whether they keep coming back is still up for negotiation. They still have much to explore, some basic questions to be answered. At this point, the most important ingredients newcomers are looking for are

—authenticity of clergy and congregation
—confidence about the pastor being the right kind of religious
   authority for times of potential crisis or times of spiritual
   doubt or uncertainty

—feeling comfortable with the theological/biblical stance of the
    congregation
—Friendship and warmth from some of the members.

Authenticity

No one wants to be a part of a group of people who are hypocriti-
cal or phony. The newcomer will be noticing whether the clergy
and congregation are made up of people who are "for real." Especially important will be the fit between what the visitor sees in the
behavior of members and what he or she hears preached from the
pulpit and spoken in classes and meetings.

If the newcomer hears people talk about love and friendship,
but perceives that this is not a very safe place to be, or that members talk *about* each other differently than when they talk *with* each
other, or that there seems to be little congruity between the faith
proclaimed and the faith lived, then he or she will not want to participate in this church.

Newcomers find authenticity (as well as religion) an awkward
topic to talk about, even with outside consultants. When we interviewed people who showed up at a church once or twice and then
never came back, they most frequently responded that the congregation seemed cold or uninviting, or else they said very little at all
about why they were not returning. When we asked them why, they
most frequently responded in a vague way, "Oh, I don't know; I
really don't have a reason; joining just didn't seem like the thing for
us." Impugning the integrity of another or the other's faith just
doesn't seem like a polite thing to do. So this most important piece
of data often gets lost.

The Pastor is the Right Kind of Authority

From our data, the way the visitor responds to the clergy seems to
be the most important factor in *first impressions* of the church. The
way the pastor shares her or his faith with the newcomer is especially important. This usually is not communicated in a one-on-one
conversation with the pastor, but comes from impressions received
from the pastor's preaching and leadership of worship.

When we are talking about the "kind of authority" the pastor
embodies, we do not mean to imply that there is a right kind of
authority for the pastor or that one authority stance is more effective than another in attracting newcomers. Different denominational
traditions, ethnic groups and social classes vary widely in their ap-
preciation of kinds and qualities of clergy authority. What is impor-

tant is that the stranger find in a church a stance toward authority with which he or she can identify and feel comfortable.

As important as clergy are for first impressions, our research showed they were not the most important factor in helping people move deeper into the life of a congregation. Members of a class or small group, or friends in the congregation rated higher than clergy in the assimilation process. The laity in the congregation seem to have most to do with whether a visitor goes beyond superficial acquaintance with the congregation. Yet, at some point in the assimilation process, newcomers need to have a favorable impression of what the clergy have to offer. Rarely do people join a congregation when they are not impressed with the clergy.

Theological and Biblical Stance of the Congregation

As with the pastor's use of his or her authority, the biblical and theological perspective of the congregation will be fundamental in helping the person who still feels like a guest feel more at home. Certainly it is the task of the church to change and enhance the newcomer's theology, but if what the stranger finds there is alien to his or her current beliefs, there is little likelihood that enough bonding will occur to cause affiliation and assimilation.

Though the pastor's use of authority and the biblical and theological stance of the congregation may be off-putting to the stranger, sometimes these matters may seem to have less prominence when positive and warm relationships develop with members of the congregation.

Warm and Friendly Relationships

More has been written about the importance of relationships to assimilation into church life in recent years (especially in main-line denominations) than about the importance of clergy authority or biblical and theological stances. It is our view that this is partly because questions about relationship to one another are easier to ask and to respond to than questions about theology and clergy authority. After all, you might be wrong about your theology, but you can't be wrong about how you feel about other people.

Even though we may not yet know which incorporation factors discussed in this chapter are more important for assimilation (or alienation), there can be no doubt that relationships are very important indeed. To quote one of the experts in the field of church growth, W. Charles Arn:

. . . a common *relationship* between the new believer and the church member is the basis upon which active membership can be established.

Numerous studies in the field of church growth indicate that the most important reason people are involved in their church today is their friendships and relationships. When people drop out of church, the reason most often given is not personal conflict in theology—it is that "I did not feel a sense of belonging. I did not feel needed, wanted, or loved." And when inactive member consider the possibility of a new church home, 75 percent tell researchers the most important thing they will look for is "the friendliness of the people." Other studies indicate that persons who become active church members will have identified an average of seven new friends in the church within the first six months. The dropouts will have made less than two.[1]

Charles Arn's father, Win Arn, makes the same point in a slightly different way in the same collection of essays. He says that there are a number of important ratios for the healthy church with regard to church growth; one of those is the friendship ratio, which he says should be 1:7:

> Each new convert or new member should be able to identify at least seven friends in the church within the first six months. Friendships appear to be the strongest bond cementing new converts or members to their congregation. If new converts do not immediately develop meaningful friendships in their church, expect them to return to their old friendships—and ways—outside the church. Seven new friendships are a minimum; ten, fifteen, or more would be better.

> There is an important time factor to this ratio, as well. The first six months are crucial. New converts or members not integrated into the body within that six-month time period are well on their way out the back door. The following chart clearly illustrates the importance of friendships established in the church during the first six months. Note that all of the fifty "Converts— Now Active Member" could name three or more friends in the church, with thirteen new members identifying seven friends, twelve identifying eight friends, and twelve listing nine friends or more. The "Dropouts" show almost the exact opposite pattern in the new friendships they established (or, more correctly, did not establish) in their church.[2]

Number of New Friends Within Six Months	0	1	2	3	4	5	6	7	8	9+	Total
Converts— Now Active Members	0	0	0	1	2	2	8	13	12	12	50
Dropouts	8	13	14	8	4	2	1	0	0	0	50

Visiting

As a part of the assimilating process in a local congregation, many churches have some kind of system for contacting or visiting those who have showed up more than once. In most of the congregations we studied, the clergy make this contact. When they were asked what role the clergy play in helping them become a member, the new joiners responded:

- 33%   A personal visit
- 23%   Effective sermons
- 19%   Private conversations in the church
- 12%   Clergy's way of conducting worship
- 5%   Crisis ministry
- 5%   Sent letters and other mailings

Especially in pastoral-sized congregations the role of clergy visits can be significant in helping people become acquainted not only with the pastor, but with the congregation as well. In this size congregation this will be a most important bonding activity.

Lay visiting, especially in the larger congregation, can also be a powerful assimilation tool. Not many churches do this. Those that do communicate to the newcomers that someone else beside the clergy are interested in their joining the parish.

Lay teams of visitors extend warm greetings from the parish and ask if the newcomers have any questions about the church or its ministry. This is a good time to ask about the newcomer's church background. If the person or family moved from another parish, they may be helped greatly by talking about their former church experience. In some cases, the newcomers are grieving the loss of their old church family and their former pastor. Encouraging them to talk about their former parish may help facilitate this grief process. It also helps them get on with new life in a new parish. This is also a time to ask them what they are looking for in a church family. Their answer to this question may help the parish visitors see that their congregation will not match this person's needs. They can then direct them to another neighborhood parish. The last question for the lay visitor to ask is, "would you like a visit from our pastor?" Some will and some won't. It certainly allows the pastor to be more selective in his/her visitation to newcomers. After the visitors' team leaves a packet of material on the parish with the newcomers, they can bid them farewell with the hope of seeing them again next Sunday at the church.

Orientation Seminars

Almost all the churches in our study had some kind of orientation process which came too late for the affiliation stage of getting acquainted with the church. They were really new member classes to which the newcomer was invited after expressing an interest in joining the church.

Different denominations and congregations use a variety of classes and seminars to help outsiders inside. Some have inquirers' classes, others new member classes, others confirmation or baptism preparation classes. In discussions of what happens to newcomers in a church we have postulated that it would be useful to make a distinction between those classes aimed at getting acquainted with the parish and those used for joining or in preparation for making a faith commitment. Get-acquainted or orientation seminars might include some of the following ideas to make them effective and useful assimilation tools.

After a person or couple returns for three to five Sundays, a congregation might assist them to become more fully oriented to the church and to its belief structure. If at least two to four newcomers attend at a time, the parish may provide a brief orientation seminar. This orientation seminar will focus only on the immediate things newcomers need to know in order to go deeper into the life of the congregation. An orientation seminar need only last for two or three sessions. It should include a tour of the building if the church plant is large. Perhaps the architecture contains symbols and history that needs explaining. Or there may be aspects of the Sunday liturgy that a newcomer will not fully understand. This is also a good time to give a brief history of the parish. When newcomers come to understand the history of a congregation, much about the new parish "falls into place." Newcomers can begin to take on some of that history and make it their history. In our study we asked the newcomers how they learned about the history of the new parish. The results were as follows:

How Did you Learn about the History of the Parish?
26%   From an adult class
25%   From clergy or church staff
17%   Still had not learned it
13%   From a friend
12%   From a parish leader
 4%   From a family member

The above statistic appears to indicate that close to 50 percent of the newcomers learned about the history of their new parishes in an intentional way. The remaining 50 percent either learned about it by accident, or they still had not learned it. The orientation seminar might be an opportunity to share this history.

This also may be an excellent time for newcomers to share their religious background. They can place their history alongside the history of the congregation. Following the sharing of histories, conversation may center on where histories are similar and where they are different. From this conversation some assumptions can be tested as to where these histories will match and where they will collide. Newcomers may be encouraged to talk about some of the things they have valued in past congregations. This will give the clergy and other church leaders a clue as to what the "psychological contract," will be between this newcomer and the parish. The term "psychological contract"[3] is discussed in Jim Anderson's book, *To Come Alive!* It refers to the unwritten, often unspoken contract that exists between each member and the congregation. It's the basic "need" or "want" that members have of their congregation. When it is broken, members become quite unhappy, but often are not articulate about what has gone awry for them. They may even begin to attack parts of congregational life not related to their psychological contract as a way of acting out their discontent. Church professionals and congregational leaders are much better off if they have some clues concerning the psychological contract between specific members and the parish.

These brief orientation seminars also may be a good time for newcomers to deal with any unresolved grief about leaving their former congregation (as we mentioned above). In all 21 congregations in our study we did not uncover one parish that took seriously the grief of newcomers over leaving their last parish. We also discovered how important an activity that really is. Some of the newcomers we interviewed had a hard time getting on with life in a new parish because their heart and soul was still somewhere else with a church community that had meant a lot to them. Even when their experience in a former congregation was not entirely positive, there are still aspects of that congregation's life that they miss. There may also be unresolved hurt or anger that prevents them from moving on to a new church relationship. In our study we discovered that churches were eager to tell the newcomers all the good and wonderful things about their congregation, but seemed unaware of the unresolved pain the newcomers had over former church experiences. A genuine ministry of caring takes place when clergy or church leaders inquire about the difficulty newcomers may have had in leaving their former church family. What is communicated is a sincere desire to take the newcomer seriously. It is saying loud and clear, "we are interested in you as a person, not just in adding you to our church roll and having another pledging unit."

And, finally, an activity which may be covered in a brief orientation session is an overview of some of the basic tenets of faith as held by congregational members. This need not be exhaustive. Its basic purpose is to give newcomers a taste of what material will be covered in the new members' class (which would come after the orientation and before joining the church). We believe all newcomers should attend such an orientation class, even if they were brought up in the denomination and have been confirmed. The material may be familiar to them, but there will be some things that will be new for these "transfers." More importantly, it gives these newcomers a chance to be together with other newcomers to the parish.

NOTES—CHAPTER V

1. W. Charles Arn, "Evangelism or Disciple-Making?", *Church Growth State of the Art*, op. cit., pp. 64-65.
2. Win Arn, op. cit., "How to Use Ratios to Effect Church Growth."
3. James D. Anderson, *To Come Alive!*, (New York: Harper and Row, 1973).

CHAPTER VI

Joining

Joining is a stage in the assimilation process when the members move from "dating" to "getting serious" about each other. This phase of the assimilation process could include the following steps (though often some of them are omitted) which struck us as similar to courtship and getting married.

Joining a Local Church	Getting Married
inviting	popping the question
formal exploration of the relationship	seeing a minister
joining	getting married

You might say that when one of the partners in a courtship "pops the question," the courtship is over. At least their relationship has moved to a different level, especially if both agree they would like to be married. There is now a new level of commitment, there is a contract, a stronger bond. Now they are engaged, a different state than before they spoke and then decided to get hitched up.

When they reach this stage, newcomers in a local church have decided to make a commitment to membership. It seems that just as often as not it is the newcomer who pops the question. Somewhere along the way these potential members have decided that this community is the best or at least a "good enough" church family for them. Or the members of the church took the initiative toward the newcomer and one or more of them asked the newcomers to join them. Here is what we learned when we asked:

"Were you invited to join by someone in the parish?"

46% Not invited by anyone
27% Were invited by the pastor or staff member.
12% Were invited by a member of the parish

4%   Were invited by a friend
2%   Were invited by a family member
7%   Were invited by another person

In other words the newcomer is as likely to take the initiative to ask the church for membership as the church is to ask the member to join. And when someone who is already in the church asks the new person to join, that someone is most likely to be a paid staff person. No matter who asks first, however, all of the churches in our study stood ready to respond with some kind of initiation program and rite once the member said yes to an invitation or took the initiative to ask to be inducted into the church. Local churches do much more by way of formal planning and implementation of joining processes after potential new members have indicated a willingness to join than they do in the earlier stages of the assimilation process. All of the congregations had some way of recognizing at least those who were joining a church for the first time and many of them had processes and rituals for people joining this particular congregation. Depending on the theological tradition and denominational background of the congregation each had a variety of rituals and processes by which they officially brought people into the life of the congregation.

Formal Exploration of the Relationship

As a part of their processes by which they officially brought people into the life of the congregation, most churches had a new member or confirmation class which the joiners were more or less expected to attend. There is a variety of discussions of new member classes available to the reader, but one of the best is that of James R. Adams and Celia Allison Hahn in their fine book *A Way to Belong*[1]. In that book they explore in depth the experiences of six members new to their congregation, St. Marks Episcopal Church in Washington DC. They list what they believe to be the tasks of the church in helping a member formally join the congregation. We will list some of them here and then briefly describe each:

Identify what people need to cope with life pressures
Encourage a concern for the prosperity of the congregation
Become clear about what kind of church you have
Help people join the congregation
Prepare people for belonging
Provide a ritual for belonging

Identify What People Need to Cope With Life Pressures

Hahn and Adams say that "people go to church . . . because they need what religious institutions historically have provided. That is, certain basic human needs can best be dealt with in what is clearly a religious arena."[2] When we asked the people who had just joined the congregations we were studying why they were joining the church, almost all of them had a story to tell about their spiritual journey, what they were looking for in a church. They were coming to the church looking for what they usually described as something that would help them cope better with themselves, their family, their job, their world. Each brought the hope that the church would provide answers or help them search. The clearer the church can be about what it is doing, about who it is trying to serve, and what the needs of these people are, the greater the possibility that those who are coming to the church looking for answers or help in their search will be able to make a meaningful decision about their participation in the congregation.

This is not to say that more people will "stay" if the church is clearer about who it is trying to serve, its identity, and what it is trying to do with its members; however, it does mean that it will make it easier, earlier in the process, for people to recognize that this congregation is not for them and that they will not be fed there. We believe that clarification of "who we are and who we are trying to serve" will reduce the attrition rate, though it may not do much to increase the joining rate of those exploring the church in the attracting and incorporating stages of assimilation into a church.

One church with which one of the authors of this paper has been working recently made a stab at identifying what the people who wanted to be members of their church "needed to cope with life pressures":

> [The people we are seeking to serve] lead a very pluralistic life style. It's filled with ambiguities and contradictions and conflicts of priorities. These tugs and pulls don't cause depressions and/ or haunting seriousness, but the life style does confuse the value system—and does set up a thirst for simplicity, peace, answers, direction. They do need and want a center point to integrate their many sided lives, to help them make sense of it all. An important and honest answer for their life. A meaning for them. This thirst is not for an authoritarian bible verse or preacher, but for an inner authority—like faith they can depend on.[3]

Here we see the church seeking to establish a serious contract with the joiner. Who are you? What do you want? What is the faith journey all about? As the church expresses and communicates through its joining processes what it is trying to do, it changes the assimilation "game." Instead of being a game which is played by people who aren't clear about what they are doing or what they have to offer, people who don't care much about who joins and what they will do after they join, the church is saying from the very start: "This is important business: it is thrilling and meaningful to us and we hope that it will be to you. If you want more of this, join us."

Encourage a Concern for the Prosperity of the Congregation

The congregations in our study got mixed reviews on communicating expectations to the joiners with regard to worship attendance, giving, theological study and reflection, prayer, service and other marks of the alive Christian. For the most part the congregations were timid at the "gate." They were not only timid about asking people to join, as we have seen above, they were also timid about asking for financial commitments to the church, and they were timid about discipleship issues in general. We asked the new members: "How were you made aware of your financial responsibilities to the congregation?" Their answers:

28%   Announcement in Sunday Worship Service
14%   Personal visit for a pledge
13%   Made known in a new member class
 5%   Pastor talked with me personally about contributing
41%   Other

The 41% response on "other" is intriguing yet confusing. Our suspicion is that, given the other four choices, little or nothing was said to these people about their financial responsibility to the church.

Here again, as with helping people clarify their contract for how the church can be helpful to them, it is important for the church to clarify what it needs to successfully implement the ministries to which it has been called.

Become clear about what kind of church you have

We have already addressed this point in the section on church identity. Here is what Hahn and Adams wrote about this issue:

The church cannot hope to attract and hold new members unless it knows what sort of church it is. A congregation that is unclear about its task and without a focus for its ministry can rarely muster the energy needed to make any visitor feel that there is any point in staying around. Only people who get some perverse pleasure from being depressed are likely to join congregations which do not have any clear reason to exist.[4]

Help People Join the Congregation

As described above, almost all the churches we studied had developed some kind of class or program to help newcomers learn about the history of the church, what the church has to offer the new person, the church's basic theological stance, and to provide newcomers an opportunity to begin to explore some of the life issues they are bringing with them into the congregation. Adams and Hahn say that the most important function here is to establish a climate of safety for the new people so that these inquirers can admit to themselves and perhaps to others that their basic needs at present are not being met. This can be the first step in authorizing people to keep taking the initiative within the life of the church in asking for help on their spiritual journey.

Provide a Ritual for Belonging

In addition to the important tasks "at the gate" described above, in almost all the congregations in our study there was some sort of formal liturgical event during the Sunday worship experience that acknowledged the joining of newcomers.

> Many congregations in the study also announced the newcomers' joining in the parish newsletter.
>
> Some posted pictures of recent joiners on the parish bulletin board.
>
> Several held additional events in honor of those who had recently joined. One congregation held a semi-annual dinner for joiners to which key leaders of the parish were invited. One large congregation held periodic luncheons in the pastor's office for groups of six to ten people so joiners had some personal time with the pastor.

Joining a congregation should be a major event in people's lives. We noted what a special event this was for Episcopalians when they joined an Episcopal congregation through the rite of confirmation. On such an occasion the Bishop usually is present and the event is quite impressive to newcomers. The opposite was true of Episcopa-

lians who joined a new congregation through letter of transfer.
When this route of joining is taken there is usually no special liturgical event in their honor. Their transfer is simply noted in the parish newsletter. It is our perception that, when congregations make
joining an important event in the life of the church and the newcomer by providing a class or classes and a special celebrative event
in the parish, they are able to draw newcomers more deeply into a
commitment.

NOTES—CHAPTER VI

1. James R. Adams and Celia Allison Hahn, *A Way to Belong*, (Washington: The
Alban Institute, Inc., 1980). Now out of print. Available as On Demand Publication.
    2. ibid., p. 58.
    3. From "St. Stephen's Communications Plan." St. Stephen's the Martyr, Edina,
MN.
    4. Adams and Hahn, p. 62.

CHAPTER VII

Going Deeper

The congregations in our study did not do a much better job with helping people go deeper into the life of the church or into their spiritual life than they did with the early stages of assimilation, attracting and incorporating. Most of the congregations had no formal system or carefully thought through plan about how one goes deeper into the faith, just as they had little or no plan to attract or incorporate people into the parish. In fact, it seemed that all formal assimilation efforts ended once people officially joined the church. Sad to say, some newcomers join a parish only to slide to its periphery, where they become inactive because there is no plan to discover their needs, no place for them to land, no help to find that place, if it exists.

By "going deeper" we mean a continuation of the discipling process of new members. Newcomers need to be encouraged and invited to get involved in a process of faith development *which the clergy and lay leadership of the congregation understand.* This could be an intellectual study of the faith, or it might include taking on or continuing a specific spiritual discipline in their lives. When we asked the new members of the churches studied if the congregation invited them to take on any personal spiritual disciplines on their own, we received these responses:

Were you invited into spiritual growth experiences through the church?

41% No
25% Retreats
20% Devotional material
11% Private Prayer
 2% Family prayer

We suspect this is part of the same dynamic of being timid at the gate and points up again the difficulty of talking about spiritual growth. As people joined the church they were not helped to become aware of their call to service or the issues of their spiritual journey. In the monograph *Religious Pilgrimage*, to which we referred in the second chapter of this book, Jean Haldane describes her experience in interviewing lay people for four hours about their spiritual journey. At first they were somewhat at a loss as to what to talk about, as they did not see themselves on a spiritual journey. Later in the interview, however, they discovered that four hours was not enough time to get in all they had to say about their journey.

A surprising finding of her research was the realization that these people did not make the connection between their spiritual journey and their life in a local parish. Haldane's interviews helped them to see more clearly the issues shaping their journey and the different pathways each was taking.

Congregations can do a great deal more to be of assistance to newcomers and all members of the parish by offering self-assessment/self-discovery events that provide insight into both one's call to ministry and the issues current in one's spiritual journey. These events can include weekend retreats, special all-day weekend events, an evening series, or perhaps a six-week series offered as an adult class on Sunday mornings.

In Roy Oswald's study of lay leader burn-out he learned that lay leaders are less likely to burn out if they are doing tasks related to their spiritual growth. Burn-out occurs more readily when members are performing tasks to which they do not feel called or in which they do not utilize their gifts or talents. In these situations where church work has no planned connection with spiritual growth, members do jobs because someone of influence asked them and they did not feel they could say "no."

More work needs to be done on the further question of how the parish can support and continually affirm members' ministries. What kind of relationship will they need with the parish clergy in order to find support for their ministry? Are there activities in the parish other than Sunday worship which can both prepare and assist them for their chosen ministry? In some cases the discernment process may uncover their call to teach a class or work on certain tasks or committees of the parish. All this is to assist members to move more deeply into the life of the spirit and service and, perhaps, into the life of their new parish—rather than simply to abandon them to their fate once they have joined the parish.

Areas of Spiritual Development in the Local Church

Going deeper as a part of the assimilation process in a local church requires some kind of theological perspective or map of what the spiritual journey is. Without it the congregation is hampered in being able to help people go further than their original commitments which led them to join a congregation. Many fine resources are available to help with this planning. Some are simple; others are complex and based on quite complicated notions of human and spiritual development. We highly recommend the work of John Westerhoff[1], Forster Freeman[2], and John Biersdorf[3] as practical models which could be applied to local church programming.

Many of these "spiritual maps", as well as others, include some kind of outline which has a developmental component; that is, it is assumed that people grow or mature or develop in the faith in a progressive way—perhaps, as Paul suggested, moving from a spiritual diet of milk to meat. Not all the schemas are developmental; some are cyclical (assuming that people move in and out of different areas of exploration and meaning as their life changes), and others seem to be either/or models which assume that you have faith or you don't (especially models of faith based on conversion as the central faith experience). Each of the various models has something to recommend it as well as profound problems that are easily discovered (and sometimes pounced on) by amateur and experienced theologians as they note the logical inconsistencies and exceptions to the processes or patterns described.

The model that some of us have been using of late is one which has six phases or eras that the spiritual pilgrim may experience. We use this model because it ties in with the steps of assimilation into a congregation that we have been using in this paper. The model does not assume that people move neatly through the "steps" from Joining, to Belonging, to Participating and so on. It is often the case that Christians skip "phases" or quite genuinely find themselves in two or more at the same time. What we are trying to do with this model is show that church members are not all in the same place with the same needs and that church programming ought to vary according to the gifts and needs of its diverse members. The model appears on the next two pages:

Areas of Spiritual Development in the Local Church

Levels of Incorporation into the Spiritual Life of the Church	Individual Behavior Related to this Area	Church Program, Ministry or Response
Joining	Taking a Confirmation or Inquirers' class	Providing a Confirmation or Inquirer's class
	Participating financially	Asking for a stewardship response
	Participating in Worship	Providing Worship
	Formally joining the church	Confirmation or joining ceremony

Belonging	Joining informal groups:
	    Sunday School
	    Fellowship groups
	    Coffee hours
	    Baseball teams
		Providing groups, classes, teams, etc.

Participating	Taking responsibility for church leadership	Providing opportunities for people to serve; recruiting, training supervising.
	Serving on a board or committee	
	Teaching Church School	
	Undertaking tasks to help at church: Every Member Canvasas, Usher, Clean Up, etc.	

Searching	Preparing for church classes	Providing prayer groups, opportunities to find and match up with spiritual friends, pastoral counseling, etc.
	Experimenting with forms of worship or meditation	
	Going to a counselor (looking for more— dissatisfied)	Referral to special groups, weekends, etc.
	Going to retreats, other churches' programs	
	Finding and working with spiritual friend or counselor	
Journeying Inward	Has a spiritual friend	Same as above and,
	Regular devotional life	Providing opportunities for leadership of Search Groups
	High self-esteem	
	Primary motive level: Actualization	
	Shares faith non-defensively	
	Celebrates life	
	Celebrates difference	
	Gives generously	
Journeying Outward	Acting in the world out of gratitude	Providing opportunities for in-depth reflection on vocation and ministry
	Working in vocation as ministry	
	Volunteer service	

This schema is meant to be a tool to help the leadership of the church carry out an analysis of those who are joining and participating in the life of a congregation, to help them get a fix on their spiritual growth needs. It will also help leaders compare needs of members with the quality of community and kind of programming in the church as it relates to the spiritual growth needs of members as well as those who are just getting acquainted with the congregation.

Let's look at the model. The model begins with "Joining." There are many who have looked at this model and said "Whoa! What about baptism (infant baptism, that is). Isn't that when most of our members 'join' the church? Doesn't the person who joins the church as an infant and grows in the church as a child start his or her spiritual growth at an earlier stage than confirmation (or for the Baptists out there, before the experience of believer's baptism)?" Well, yes, we reply; you're right about that, and for those folks who are coming back to the church after having been raised there and going through the Christian Education program, we really should call this category "Re-joining."

What we found in our study was that the vast majority of people who were coming back to the church and needing to be assimilated into it were individuals who had indeed already been in church, who had had a good experience in the church as young people, and who were looking for ways to get back in. Few of the newcomers to the growing congregations in our study were people who had not had experience with church in the past and were joining a local congregation for the first time.

The vast majority of the people in our study were new to this congregation, had experience with church in the past, and were at a place in their lives where they were looking for something new. There was a new curiosity in them, a new hope that the church would help them (or their children) in a special way, a particular need (some had just lost a loved one, or a job—others were experiencing a profound life change such a marriage, the birth of a child, a move to a new community). In other words newcomers are coming to the church with a readiness to experience what the church has to offer and a hope that it will be of help to them at this special time in their lives.

When people are in the process of choosing and joining a congregation, they "get active" in certain ways. They are curious and they begin to explore. They go to church first to worship; they begin to talk with members about their experience at the church; they take inquirers classes, orientation classes; or confirmation classes; and sometimes they get involved in other ongoing church classes or programs to find out what these folks believe, what people who are members here do.

It is important to note that at this stage the major motivators are likely to be curiosity and belonging. For most newcomers there will not be a strong understanding of their own faith needs, what they need to grow, and how they can contribute (except by participation in worship and stewardship).

We found that as members "get in" to the church (this may well be before they formally join the congregation) their needs for belonging and inclusion become stronger than their curiosities and faith questions. After people feel that they have "gotten in," (and this is usually after having formally joined the church) they look for ways to belong. That is, they want to be known by some of the other members and they want to know other members. They join and become active in groups. These may be classes, choirs, teams, clubs, prayer groups, etc. At this point there is a connection in the mind of the growing Christian between faith and belonging. Being a good church member is having friends at church. Being a Christian is being in community. For some this is where their faith journey stops. They have friends; they have community; they worship on Sunday; they "help" financially and with their time, when asked.

Some members move into another phase of involvement (which may not decrease their Belonging activities) we call Participation. This is a busier kind of taking part. Here people don't just respond when asked, they take initiative. They notice when things need doing and they do what is required. They are most likely on a board or committee, teaching a class, and/or in a position of trust with regard to the church books, money raising, or making sure the church is heated for Sunday morning worship.

These dimensions of growth are important and worthy steps into Christian community and responsibility. They may accompany or stand apart from three other levels of incorporation into the faith: Searching, Journeying Inward, and Journeying Outward. It is interesting to note that some who find themselves in these later three areas of faith development have little or nothing to do with the former (Joining, Belonging, and Participating) and some are "into" both.

Searching people are often an annoyance to clergy and other church leaders. They are asking questions; they are often challenging the leadership, the practice, even the faith. These people are often searching in and out of the church for answers and help. They might belong to a Bible study or prayer group at another church. They may take many opportunities to participate in retreats, special study groups, pilgrimages which will help them on their faith journey. People at this stage of faith development are not likely to stay long with one "solution" to their intellectual and faith questions, though they may be quite dogmatic for a time about one orthodoxy or another as they try it out.

The key to recognizing yourself or another at this "stage" of faith development is the testing or experimental nature of one's thought and practice. Those practicing meditation try yoga for a while, then Zen, then Herb Benson's relaxation technique; those intellectually searching will find themselves committed to Nietzsche, then to Tillich, then to the New Testament with no interpreters. There is a kind of dissatisfaction that characterizes the Searcher. The dissatisfaction may be cloaked in dogmatic positions (because I am uncertain about my position, I will have to defend and protect what I have arrived at so far, so as to not be too badly shaken) or it may be a quite open and forthright search for "what works best for me."

The best place to start in working with members who may be ready to move into the Searching phase or from it into that of Journeying would most likely be to ask these members to identify a ministry to which they felt called, whether in the church or in the world. Almost all of the growth models currently in use (or perhaps we should more accurately say, "in discussion") in main line churches assume that part of going deeper is helping members discover their vocation (lay ministry). Lay ministry is the way we express our faith through the way we live and work in the world. Verna Dozier's book, *The Authority of the Laity*[4] could be an excellent resource for helping laity gain clarity on this issue. To what extent do they feel called by God to their daily occupation? . . .or to being a certain kind of person at their place of work? Another excellent resource for helping people find their calling through a small group study process are Volumes I and II of *Support for Laity in Their Ministries*.[5]

Whereas Searching is rooted in uncertainty, Journeying Inward and/or Outward is rooted in assurance. Having tested many avenues without knowing where one was going as a Searcher, the Journeyer has a confidence that though the goal may not be clearly in view, the journey will be safe and meaningful. The Journeyer is more likely to have settled into a practice than is the Searcher. The Journeyer is comfortable with his or her spiritual practice, ready to learn from others, but not needing to grasp at the next new thing because of dissatisfaction with what he or she is now doing. The person at the Journeying "stage" is interested in how others are different, not because he or she wants to change or convert them, but rather to learn from their experience. In other words, he or she comes at faith in a non-anxious way, open and exploring, interested, but not as "needy."

Some people at the Journeying "stage" focus more on the inward life—the life of prayer, their own psychological development, the life of faith, others tend to focus more on the outward life—the life of compassion, doing for others, responding to injustice in appropriate and non-anxious ways, acting in their vocation out of a sense of mission and call rather than simply as a way to get money.

Some of the journeyers at this "stage" are active in their local congregations, others are not. Belonging, Participating, and Searching activities are not necessarily characteristic of people who are Journeying Inward or Outward. These activities are not mutually exclusive, but it may be that those who are working on their Journey Inward or Outward have turned from the busyness of Participation or the groupiness of Belonging.

Our point in this schema is that assimilation is not just a matter of Joining, Belonging or Participating, but that assimilation into the faith includes the next steps of the journey into Searching and Journeying Inward and Outward.

A review of where newcomers and members alike are on their journey will help the leaders of the church ask not only what are the needs of the individual who is being assimilated into the church, but also what is it that the church is providing for those who wish to take the next steps in faith. Are there programs or ministries which will help the member who is at a Searching phase of her or his life? And what of those who are Journeying Outward and/or Inward? What resources are available at the church to help them? Moreover, what are the church's values with regard to people who have found that their ministry is *primarily* outside the local congregation? Does the church psychologically commission them to be about the work of Christ in the world, or does the church de-commission them by looking down its collective nose at those who have moved from Participation to the Journey Inward?

NOTES—CHAPTER VII

1. John Westerhoff, *Will our Children Have Faith*, (New York: Seabury, 1976).

2. Forster Freeman, *Readiness for Ministry Through Spiritual Direction*, (Washington: The Alban Institute, 1986).

3. John Biersdorf, *Healing of Purpose: God's Call to Discipleship*, (Nashville: Abingdon, 1985).

4. Verna Dozier, *The Authority of the Laity*, (Washington: The Alban Institute, 1982).

5. Celia Hahn, James Adams, Anne Amy and Barton Lloyd, *My Struggle to be a Caring Person: Support for Laity in their Ministries, Vol. I*, and *What Do I Have to Offer?: Support for Laity in their Ministries, Vol. II*, (Washington, The Alban Institute).

CHAPTER VIII

Where Do We Go from Here?

Learnings for Churches from the Research Process

The reader has learned something about assimilation of new members in earlier chapters and may well be asking herself or himself at this point, "How are we doing in our church with regard to the assimilation of new members into the congregation?" From what we have learned about churches that are successful in assimilating new members into their congregations, it would not make a great deal of sense to do an institutional audit of your congregation starting with an assessment of your recruiting system, then moving to your greeting systems and on to what provision is made to help people join and get incorporated into the life of the church. Rather, we propose that you start with getting information about your church and the way it functions with regard to newcomers by talking to the newcomers themselves about their experience. Then worry about what systems and structures you have in place for assimilation, if you need to.

The Difficulties of Interviewing Your Own Members

All kinds of learning occurs when one sets out to do research. Sometimes the discoveries that come have little to do with the content of the particular study itself. Such was the case when we addressed ourselves to the topic of assimilation in congregations. When we started this project we knew we would have trouble getting the kind of information we wanted if we allowed people from the parishes we were studying to interview newcomers to their own congregations. When people interview someone they know or with whom they have an ongoing relationship, there is sometimes a reticence in the interviewer, the interviewee, or both, to explore as fully as they might some of the themes and experiences that are crucial to understand if one is to explore in any depth the issue of assimilation. For example, what if an interviewee had a rather awkward experience with the interviewer's mother on the second Sunday he attended? He may not want to tell that story, or he may want to sugarcoat it so not to embarrass the interviewer or impede their developing relationship.

Moreover, when you interview someone you know, there is a tendency to think that you already know the answers to some of the questions. Instead of asking Bill directly his impressions of the pastor, you may remember what he as said before, or how his wife describes Bill's feelings about the pastor. So, you don't ask—or you don't probe if you get evasive or shallow answers.

Further, as an interviewer and also a member of the congregation, you may realize that some of the things Bill is complaining about you could have done something about; you may feel guilty that you didn't speak to him on the first day he and his family attended church. Or you may become annoyed that Bill didn't come to the coffee hour after church and instead held back as if he were testing the church's ability to be friendly.

As we mentioned earlier, it is not easy for many people to talk within their congregational community about spiritual and religious matters. They seem too personal and private for people to share them easily, and a kind of "conspiracy of silence" develops. "The conspiracy of silence" certainly is abetted by the fact that much of what happens in one's spiritual journey takes place in those parts of the brain where language to describe it does not reside. Michael Gazzaniga's[1] research leads him to believe that humans do not have a linear, unified conscious experience and that their thought processes do not proceed serially. Rather, he says, the brain is organized into relatively independent functioning units that work in parallel ways, frequently apart from our conscious verbal selves. He writes:

> What I am suggesting is that the normal human is called upon to interpret real actions and to construct a theory as to why they have occurred. That would be a trivial matter if everything we did was the product of very conscious action; in that case, the source of the behavior is known before the action occurs. I argue that the normal person does not possess a unitary conscious mechanism where the conscious system is privy to the sources of all his or her actions. I think that the normal brain is orga-

nized into modules and that most of these modules are capable of actions, moods, and responses. All except one work in the non-verbal ways such that their method of expression is solely through overt behavior or more covert emotional reactions.[2]

Therefore, what goes on in one part of our experience we may not be able to put words to or express clearly and rationally. Thus, we find ourselves in an embarrassing position with our fellow Christian when we can't make good arguments for what we think or what we believe about God and the nature of religious experience.

"The conspiracy of silence," as we said earlier, has become a part of the organizational norms of the mainline, liberal church. For all these reasons, it is not only difficult for members to interview newcomers from the same congregation, it is not likely that they will get very good data. There is another problem with members of a congregation interviewing their own folk: it is difficult for them to report what is learned to members of the congregation who might be able to do something about it (a church board or evangelism committee or greeting committee). We have found that the inter-viewers are uncomfortable sharing some of what they have learned with the leadership, and those who lead often find it difficult to hear what they have to say. The interviewers from the same congre-gation know how hard people try to make their church an attractive and welcoming place. They know all the effort that has gone into setting up teams to call on people and getting greeters for Sunday morning. Further, the leaders of the church know what a chore this has all been. When someone comes along, again, telling them how they fall short, they don't want to hear it—especially from another member of the congregation.

Bringing in an Interviewer from the Outside

When we brought people in who were neighbors, who had a little training in doing interviewing, and who were particularly interested in the subject of how people become assimilated into the life of a congregation, energy was generated that would not have been pres-ent using "internal" resources.

Those who were being interviewed were excited about being taken seriously and invited to talk in depth about their experience. The fact that the interviewers were outsiders gave the message that the people being interviewed were very important and that the pro-cess was serious. It wasn't just another instance of the church trying half-heartedly to figure out what they were up to. This was special research that would help the congregation, and, perhaps, would help other churches as well.

The interviewers were also excited by this process. As they got close to people and their motivations for church participation, they learned a great deal. This process generated a dialogue for which both the interviewers and the interviewees were hungry. These interviewers cared about the church and were vitally interested in how it worked. Newcomers were especially interesting to talk to because they were *thinking* about their church experience. They were not participating out of habit—they were on a search, they had a need, something was missing from their lives and they came to this institution attentive to how it would treat them and whether or not it would provide anything important to them. Likewise, the interviewers were not people who were merely doing their duty. They wanted to get close to people, to find out about their spiritual journeys, and what happened to them when they entered into the church for their personal development. The interviewers were paid nothing for their work (except their out-of-pocket expenses). They gladly interviewed 15 to 20 people, spent hours analyzing the data from face-to-face interviews as well as written questionnaires, wrote a 20- to 30- page report, and then went back to the church several times to help the leaders of the congregation understand what they had written. Even with all this work, most of the interviewers said they wanted to do more. It was fun! They learned from the experience. The interviewing was meaningful in itself.

Not only was the experience a positive one for the persons interviewed and those interviewing, it was also a positive one for the leaders of the congregations. They listened attentively to what was learned from the consultants. They sought to incorporate the consultants' suggestions into the way they dealt with newcomers. They felt they were really getting something, and they were. The fact that these volunteer consultants were from outside the congregation gave them an increased edge of authority which empowered everyone to take their suggestions a little more seriously than they might have otherwise.

How This Process Can Be Used in Other Situations

All this leads us to suggest several ways to begin incorporating some of the learning from this report into your congregation:

Read the Report

Going through this report and getting hold of some of the concepts that are relevant to the assimilation process will help you reflect on some of the areas in which you will want to do research in your congregation. Other texts you might want to review are listed in the bibliography: at this point, let us recommend Lyle Schaller's book,

Assimilating New Members, Carl Dudley's book, *Where Have All The People Gone*, Dean Hoge and David Roozen's book, *Understanding Church Growth and Decline*, and Bob Gribbon's excellent monographs *Half The Congregation: Ministry With 18 To 40 Year Olds* and *When People Seek the Church.*

Is More Data Needed about What Happens to Newcomers at Your Church?

Once you have reviewed this manual and some of the other material listed above, you will want to ask some specific questions about the state of the assimilation processes in your congregation. Even if you think you know well what happens to newcomers in your congregation, you will find it much easier to "sell" ideas about improving your system if you have first-hand information from people who have just been through the joining process. You can get this information by interviewing the people who are responsible for welcoming and assimilating new people *and* by interviewing those who have recently come in.

If it seems that more information is needed about what happens to newcomers at your church, you will want to get the support and approval of your official board to go ahead with a process to study the assimilation of newcomers. It is usually a good idea to get the board's approval in principle before inviting another church to join you, and then to give the board a specific outline of how you will proceed before actually starting the interviewing.

Invite Another Church to Join You

Based on the reasoning above, we would suggest that you not try to do this interviewing yourselves. Rather, we would urge you to invite another congregation to join with in such a way that you can swap interviewing, analyzing, and feedback services. That is, you might invite another congregation of your denomination to identify four or five people who would be willing to become consultants to your church and you would identify four or five people who could become consultants to theirs. This will resolve the problems of interviewing in your own church. This process will work best if the church you are considering working with meets these qualifications:

- It is approximately the same size. The dynamics of church life in different sized congregations are substantially different.
- It is of the same denomination. The differences between churches based on their denominational ties can be quite striking. It would take the consultants a good deal of time and

effort just to learn the structure, let alone become familiar with the culture of that denomination.

- It is of the same cultural group.
- It has similar values regarding evangelism and religious expression.

Devise a Process to be Used in both Churches

Once you have a partner congregation with which to exchange consulting services, it would be wise for the two groups of consultants to develop a process for interviewing and analyzing the two congregations. This is a task that the two groups can do together. The rest of the tasks will need to be done separately to avoid the problems we have indicated above. Together the two groups can outline a plan which should include answers to these questions:

What will we study? What will we look for in the assimilation process?

How can we find out what we *think* we are doing to assimilate new members, and then find out what we are actually doing?

Do our consultants have enough background in interviewing to do this job without an initial training experience? If not, what kind of joint training can be arranged?

What questions shall we include in our interviews? (Appendix B includes a list of questions similar to those the Alban Institute used in the research that is being reported here.)

What processes will be used to collate and analyze the information we gather from the interviews?

Who will decide which newcomers to interview in each church? In churches with less than 150 people worshipping on Sunday morning, we recommend that an attempt be made to identify and interview all the people who have visited for the first time and then attended church more than two times in the last three years (this, of course, would include the dropouts as well as the joiners, the active as well as the inactive). In congregations with more than 150 on Sunday morning, interview at least twenty people who have come to church for the first time within the last two years and have become active and ten people who have come to church for the first time within the last two years, but have dropped out.

Who will invite them to the interviews?

Do the Interviews

We found that the interviews went best when they were done at the church in a private place. They lasted between an hour and an hour and a half. Also, it is better to interview individuals, not couples. In several of the consulting teams the interviewers met with their interviewees in different rooms *simultaneously*. A coordinator of the interviewing process called the newcomers, set up the appointment, and told the people when and where they would be met.

Analyze the Information

Once the interviewing is complete, the interviewers will want to collate all the information they have gathered in response to each question. The interviewers can then look for themes in the information, problems that people have experienced, the strengths of the assimilation processes already in place, and the quality of experience of the newcomers.

Write a Report

A well written report will have an outline similar to this:

Introduction
   Overall description of the process
   Who gathered the information
   From whom the information was gathered (in general, no names)
A description of what the church currently has undertaken to do to help newcomers feel welcome and become assimilated
A description of what actually happens, in general, to people when they first arrive at the church and on their first several visits
The strengths of the current process
The weaknesses of the current process
Recommendations for improving the process

Give the Report Verbally and in Writing

A written report has much less power than an oral one. In talking with people about what has been learned you can clarify where they do not understand: you can convey excitement, enthusiasm and hope that is sometimes lost on the written page, and you can correct and modify as you go along if your reporting is not one hundred percent on target. It is also true that a verbal report has more authority and staying power if it is backed up by a written report. Your findings will have much more clout if you write them and share them verbally with those you hope will be able to implement your recommendations.

Resolving the Issue of Whether or Not to Grow

There is usually a price tag attached to the decision to grow. Congregations need to become more acutely aware of the price growth requires before the decision will have any meaning. Of course, every parish wants to grow—but on its own terms. It wants to add people to its pledge list and attendance sheets without change or effort. Not infrequently congregations perceive the internal changes that need to take place in order to grow, and will ultimately reject those changes because the price is too high. They would rather not grow than face changes like these:

—having to get acquainted with new people
—doing away with a white, male hierarchy's stamp of approval on every major decision
—accommodating to new ideas
—allowing underprivileged neighborhood children to attend the day school in their church building
—changing their attitude towards singles, minorities, the elderly, gays, the unemployed, blue collar workers, welfare recipients, etc.

Most congregations have unwritten standards of acceptability. If newcomers do not measure up to those standards, they will have little chance of feeling fully accepted by the congregation. Congregations that are serious about growth usually need to confront some serious problems related to their own internal life and identity. They may need to seek outside assistance to help keep their feet to the fire when tough changes are demanded. Once some of these internal changes are accomplished they can begin doing work on new member ministries. Seen from a positive perspective, a serious decision to grow is a serious decision to parish renewal and revitalization.

Church Growth and Church Priorities

Quite likely the reader has read somewhere before reading this book that if you want your church to grow, you must make growth the number one priority in the life of the church. It seems to us, both from our research and from our values about what churches are supposed to be, that making growth the number one priority for a congregation misses the point. There are three concerns that need to be raised about making church growth your number one priority.

In the first place it seems to us that those who are concerned about growth as the number one priority put the emphasis in the Great Commission[3] in the wrong place. They look first at the word "all" and think they will be measured on the numbers they have brought in. Perhaps there would be an advantage to looking first at the words "make disciples" and worrying more about the kind of baptizing and teaching they are doing and less about the numbers being procured. Perhaps the focus on numbers makes for a wide door (when a narrow one might be better) and an easy entry, and a fairly quick discovery that there is not much here that is of interest to the newcomer. Perhaps the focus on getting people in and holding them misses the point. What is needed is a religious experience that helps people grow and develop more than one which is attractive to many. And perhaps, just perhaps, the religious experience of quality will mean more in the long run than the religious experience of quantity.

Second, as we studied these churches that *were* successful in terms of numbers we did not find that they focused on growth as a priority or that they paid much attention to helping people get in. They had found something that worked. They made themselves attractive by attending to the task of being the church, not soliciting, seducing, or even "greasing the skids" for those who showed up once or twice. Healthy churches are attractive places; they draw people to them; they grow. Not, apparently, because they work at growth, but because they work at ministry. Those who want to be a part of that kind of community will find a way to get in.

Finally, it seems to us that too much attention to growth is a good way to avoid paying attention to what it means to be faithful. The church can get all caught up in recruiting, welcoming, and assimilating and lose sight of the fact that there may be little there which will nourish those who come to feed.

So, our advice is to pay attention first to who you are as a church. What is your ministry? What difference are you trying to make in the lives of those who are members and those in need of the church's ministry? As you do this, observe what is being done or not being done that assists a seeker's progress into the journey of faith. Then you will have your assimilation priorities in order.

Summary

Let's think back about the most important themes of this book.

The most powerful factors that are likely to enhance or inhibit church growth are out of the control of those who would like to bring growth about in the congregation. They are environmental factors such as neighborhood change and church attendance patterns in the larger society.

However, there are a number of things that the church can do from inside to help promote growth, even in situations where the environmental factors are clearly stacked against the congregation. Most important are:

A clear identity
Congregational harmony and cooperation
A pastor who generates enthusiasm
A warm and inviting welcome
A place to land.

These and the many other ideas and techniques discussed in this book will help. But nothing will substitute for the enthusiasm the members have for the Christian faith. The sure knowledge that "Christ has died, Christ is risen, Christ will come again" is so contagious that it can hardly be stifled by the clumsiest of organizations, the most taciturn of members, the most inarticulate of pastors. Somehow God will break through it all, and the newcomer will discover—perhaps, in spite of the church—the message that God is in the midst of life and the Christian church is one place where the believer can join with others in a community of belonging, participating, searching and journeying.

NOTES—CHAPTER VIII

1. Michael S. Gazzaniga, *The Social Brain: Discovering the Networks of the Mind*, (New York: Basic Books, 1985).

2. —-, "The Social Brain," *Psychology Today*, (November, 1985):32.

3. Matthew 28:19, "Go therefore and make disciples of all nations, baptizing them in the name of the Father and of the Son and of the Holy Spirit, teaching them to observe all that I have commanded you; and lo, I am with you always, to the close of the age."

All Saints Episcopal Church's Assimilation Plan

While we were in the process of writing this paper, long after the data gathering and analysis had been done, one of us was working as consultant to All Saints Episcopal Church in Pasadena, California. Patrick Thyne and Neil Warren, lay persons in that congregation, had written a paper on the assimilation process they wanted for their parish which they shared with us at the time of that consultation. With their permission we are sharing that paper with you here because it is an excellent summary of how the ideas we have been sharing with you in this paper can fit into a working plan for the incorporation process in a local church.

Not all of these ideas have been tried at All Saints. Some have been tried and didn't go exactly as planned, others have been "in place" for years, and, of course, some have recently been started and are highly successful as a part of the congregation's assimilation process.

All Saints is a corporation size church, and some of the ideas that are discussed here are not practically possible for smaller congregations. And some of them may not be practically possible for other larger congregations—such as the rector calling every newcomer on the phone once or twice a year—but the ideas here are fully congruent with the thesis of this book and the learning derived from our research.

If you are not familiar with Episcopal jargon, there are two words it may help to define. The "vestry" is the governing board of the congregation. The "rector" is the senior pastor.

The rest of this chapter is the text from the All Saints paper.

From the Parking Lot to the Vestry

One Person's 5-Year Encounter With All Saints Church (Including Divine Interjections)

Katherine Simpson is a 37-year-old woman who lives in Eagle Rock. Her two children, Chris (a 10-year-old boy) and Jenny (an 8-year-old girl) are in the fourth and second grade at Eagle Rock Elementary School.

Katherine has been separated from her husband, Lew, for three years, and their divorce has been final for two. While her parents and an older sister live in Eagle Rock and are highly supportive of her, and while she has two or three close friends, Katherine is a lonely, frustrated, and frightened woman. The last three years have been miserable for her, though not as horrendous as the last three years of the marriage. Lew had a severe drinking problem, and toward the end of the marriage he regularly abused Katherine and the children both physically and emotionally.

One of Katherine's two or three closest friends, Sally Edwards, has attended All Saints Episcopal Church in Pasadena since she was a child. Katherine met Sally two years ago when their children were both in kindergarten in Eagle Rock. Sally is well aware of Katherine's loneliness and frustration, and Sally has on several occasions invited Katherine to special events at All Saints. Sally has been eager for Katherine to get involved in the Church because, having gone through a similar set of family circumstances, Sally has long felt that the programs at All Saints have met her needs.

On this particular Sunday morning Katherine wakes up early. The week has been long and heavy, and Saturday night's sleep is fitful. Somewhere around three in the morning she decides that something new has to happen in her life. She remembers Sally's invitation to give All Saints Church a try. Checking Saturday's Los Angeles Times for the Sunday schedule, she decides to attend the 8:30 a.m. service. She wakes Chris and Jenny, tells them what she has in mind, and combines an invitation with a hard sell designed to get them to accompany her to the Church.

> I FIRST SPOKE THESE WORDS TO JEREMIAH, BUT THEY APPLY NOW TO YOU, KATHERINE, AS SURELY AS THEY ONCE DID TO THE PROPHET: "BEFORE I FORMED YOU IN THE WOMB, I KNEW YOU, AND BEFORE YOU WERE BORN I CONSECRATED YOU; I APPOINTED YOU TO BE A WITNESS." YOU DON'T KNOW IT YET, KATHERINE, BUT YOU SOON WILL: YOUR DESTINY AND MINE ARE INTIMATELY INTERWOVEN.

As Katherine Simpson drives toward Pasadena on that Sunday morning with her two kids in the back seat, she is filled with all kinds of ambivalence. She feels good about the fact that she is finally trying something which may bring some meaning to her life, but she is frankly scared to death at the prospect of "going to church," being with so many strangers, and trying to seem so put together. It has been years since she attended the Catholic Church of her youth, and she is not at all sure what to expect. All she knows is that her life turned gray a few years ago, and she hasn't been able to bring it alive again. She hasn't felt very worthwhile or needed or cared for for a long time. And whether she is consciously aware of it or not, that is what she is desperately seeking from this frightening Sunday morning adventure.

There are thousands of persons like Katherine Simpson within a 15-mile radius of All Saints Episcopal Church. They have found life overwhelmingly difficult, and their condition is close to critical when it comes to feeling good about themselves. If each of these persons could somehow sense that she deeply matters, and that there is nothing that can happen to change that fact, perhaps she could discover the security she so desperately seeks.

Unfortunately, most of these persons experience themselves as of limited value in a consistently cold and uncaring world. They often reach out for help from life stories that are filled with emptiness and hopelessness. They are looking for something revolutionary—to be loved for no good reason at all, to be cared for without conditions, to be appreciated just for who they are, to be linked up with other people who are trying desperately to find something better and more deeply satisfying.

I suspect that the church's most critical task involves the early months of encounter with these people—welcoming them into a loving fellowship, nurturing them delicately and thoroughly for the first five years, and then calling them to the task of providing a similar kind of experience for others who will wake up one Sunday morning desperately lonely and eager to try something new. If the church can make the first five years of Katherine Simpson's experience at All Saints Church stimulating, meaningful, and filled with warmth and caring, she may well be motivated to weave her life into our lives and move in concert with us toward a goal fundamentally Christian in nature.

I would like to suggest ten steps in this five-year process of helping persons move from loneliness to leadership.

AND I WOULD LIKE TO SUPPORT, IN THESE BRACKETED INTERJECTIONS, WHAT I HAVE IN MIND FOR KATHERINE AND THIS CHURCH AS SHE PROCEEDS THROUGH THIS PROCESS.

(1) Before They Choose To Attend

I believe our goal should be to project a balanced image in our community involving worship, outreach, and caring. I suspect, however, that most persons will be attracted to our church because they think it may be a place in which they can find themselves needed, cared for, and made to feel worthwhile.

There are three ways in which we will be able to convey the idea that All Saints has a caring dimension.

> I WANT YOU TO BE VERY CAREFUL WITH THIS PART OF THE PROCESS. WHAT YOU'RE DOING HERE IS NOT MARKETING ALL SAINTS CHURCH, BUT BEARING WITNESS ON MY BEHALF. THIS IS NOT ADVERTISING, BUT INVITATION.

A. Our advertisements in the newspaper should adopt some kind of slogan that involves the caring image—e.g., "All Saints— Where We care For The World's People. . .Including You."

B. All of our literature should incorporate the idea that it matters significantly to us that people attend our Church and become involved with us.

C. Perhaps we need to encourage our members to invite their friends "to come and be a part of our caring company," "to tell them how much we desire their involvement with us," and to generally let these friends know of our commitment to the idea that all persons are genuinely loveable and worthwhile.

> O, GO AHEAD, CALL IT WHAT IT IS: *EVANGELISM*. WHY HAVE YOU GIVEN THIS TASK TO THE FUNDAMENTALISTS? I HAVE PEOPLE IN MIND—LOTS OF KATHERINES—WHO ARE WAITING FOR A PERSONAL INVITATION TO VISIT ALL SAINTS CHURCH. THAT'S FUNDAMENTAL!

(2) Parking Lot

Many successful Church builders have advanced the idea that the way we treat visitors when they enter our parking lot has a significant impact on their sense of how we feel about them.

> PARKING LOTS! I WHO CREATED THE HEAVENS AND THE EARTH MUST NOW ATTEND TO PARKING LOTS! DOES THAT SURPRISE YOU? ACTUALLY, IT'S NOTHING NEW. REMEMBER THE DETAILS FOR NOAH'S ARK AND THE FIRST TEMPLE? I'VE BEEN ATTENDING TO THE DETAILS FOR MILLENNIA, BECAUSE THE DETAILS MATTER, ESPECIALLY WHEN WE'RE DEALING WITH TENTATIVE PEOPLE WHO, EVEN AS THEY COME TO- WARD US, ARE LOOKING FOR REASONS TO STAY AWAY.

It seems to me that our parking lots need to have highly visible signs indicating everything people need to know about parking there. The lines for the spaces need to provide enough room for people to park comfortably, not just for the sake of their car doors but primarily because it is an announcement of how well we have planned for their arrival, and thus a sign about how much we care about their coming.

And I wonder if we don't need to have persons assigned to the parking lots, as many churches do, whose function is to be helpful by directing people to available spaces, answering their questions, greeting them in a friendly way, making sure that their needs are met, and generally conveying the message that we are a church that cares.

AND HOW ABOUT A SUPPLY OF UMBRELLAS FOR THOSE IN-ADVERTENT SUNDAY RAINS, FOR WHICH, IN ADVANCE, I APOLOGIZE.

(3) That First Sunday in Church

If we care enough, we will make sure that from the moment a person reaches the church door until they are driving down the street toward home, their experience is one of feeling cared about.

DIP INTO YOUR MEMORY FOR A MOMENT. WHO DO YOU FIND THERE WHO FIRST TALKED WITH YOU ABOUT ME? ON THE FINGERS OF YOUR LEFT HAND, COUNT FIVE PEOPLE— YES, USE YOUR THUMB!—WHO FIRST IMPRESSED UPON YOU THE NOTION THAT THE CHURCH IS A PLACE THAT CARES FOR YOU. THIS ISN'T AN EXERCISE IN NOSTALGIA. THOSE PEOPLE WERE MY ONLY WAY OF GETTING TO YOU. NOW I'VE SENT KATHERINE TO ALL SAINTS, AND SHE'S GOING TO EN-COUNTER THERE MEN AND WOMEN AND CHILDREN WHO WILL GIVE HER WHATEVER IMPRESSIONS SHE WILL HAVE OF ME. SO YOU CAN IMAGINE HOW MUCH I HAVE AT STAKE WITH HER ON THIS INITIAL SUNDAY. TREAT HER, PLEASE, WITH GREAT CARE.

I think of three places on that first Sunday where this may happen most effectively:

A. When the ushers pass a program to Katherine as she enters, it would be reassuring if they could emotionally move toward her by greeting her with a smile and a friendly word. It doesn't much matter whether Katherine is a first-timer or an old-timer, it just feels good to experience a warm welcome. Moreover, if these ushers could have signs pinned on them that say something like "ASK ME IF YOU HAVE A QUESTION," and if they could answer virtually any reasonable question (e.g., "Where are the classes for Chris—age 10—and Jenny—age 8?"), they could perform a very valuable service and begin to create a highly caring atmosphere.

B. Perhaps there are ways in which the process of passing the peace could become a more effective means of transmitting caring in the congregation. Maybe the peace could be passed earlier in the service so that newcomers would feel more involved with the people around them during the service. And maybe the peace could include instructions to ask some very innocuous question like, "How long have you attended this church?" And perhaps "old members" could be encouraged to make visitors feel especially welcome and to answer any of the questions they might have about participation in the worship experience.

C. When the pastor makes the announcements, perhaps he could be even more aware that there are 15 or 20 Katherine Simpsons in the audience—dying to be cared for, needing to feel needed, desperate for some sense of mattering.

(4) First-Year Periodic Involvement

However impressed Katherine Simpson may be on that first Sunday morning, she probably will not proceed toward membership for a year or so. During that first year in which she attends now and then, the decision about whether she will choose to weave her life into the life of the congregation will likely hang in the balance. If we act coolly toward her, she may well maintain all the anonymity her shyness dictates. And her involvement may remain periodic five years later. But if we pursue the goal of letting her know in every possible way that we exist for the purpose of transmitting a *personal* and revolutionary Gospel filled with unconditional love, then we will reach out to Katherine as warmly, attractively, and often as we know how.

IN KATHERINE'S LIFE, AS I SEE IT, THIS IS THE YEAR OF THE EUCHARIST. I DON'T CARE IF SHE LEARNS TO SPELL THE WORD, OR EVER HEARS IT; BUT DURING HER FIRST YEAR AT ASC, I WANT HER TO EXPERIENCE WHAT EUCHARIST MEANS. ON HER FIRST SUNDAY, SHE'LL BE COMPARING IT TO HER

CATHOLIC PAST, AND WONDERING WHEN TO STAND AND
WHEN TO KNEEL AND WHEN I STOPPED SPEAKING IN LATIN.
AS THE YEAR PROGRESSES, I WANT HER TO DISCOVER THAT
THE EUCHARIST IS NOT JUST A LITURGY, IT IS A MEAL, FOOD
FOR HER SOUL. AND I WANT HER TO FIND THIS MEAL PRE-
CISELY IN WHAT WE CALL "THE MYSTERY: CHRIST HAS DIED,
CHRIST IS RISEN, CHRIST WILL COME AGAIN." I WANT HER TO
LEARN THAT IN HIS DEATH, I LOVE HER WITHOUT CONDI-
TION OR QUALIFICATION; THAT BECAUSE OF HIS RESURREC-
TION, SHE CAN TRUST THAT SOMEONE IS IN CHARGE IN THE
MIDST OF WHAT SEEMS TO HER NOW TO BE CHAOS, BOTH
WITHIN AND AROUND HER; AND THAT THE PROMISE OF HIS
COMING AGAIN OPENS THE DOOR TO THE FUTURE AND
GIVES HER A LIVELY HOPE. AS YOU WORK WITH HER DURING
THIS FIRST YEAR, REMEMBER THAT FOR HER, IT IS THE YEAR
OF THE EUCHARIST.

A. Members of the vestry are essentially, if I understand cor-
rectly, shepherds of the flock. It would be tremendously helpful if
Katherine Simpson were assigned a shepherd or a person from a
shepherd's team to care for her during this year of periodic involvement. If this shepherd could contact Katherine on Sunday morning
or by telephone on a regular basis and indicate to her that this
church desires to meet her needs, to answer her questions, to reach
out and help in every way possible, could she keep from experiencing caring?

B. If the pastor or a member of his staff could call her on the
phone once or twice during the year, write her one or two letters
on the basis of information received from her shepherd, have his
picture taken with her and her kids in the courtyard, even visit in
her home, she would feel another source of caring.

C. If the shepherd would make sure that she is placed on the
mailing list and if she were invited to all-church events specifically
related to her interests, this would be a third way to convince here
of our concern.

(5) New Members Class

When Katherine decides that she wants to be a member of the
church, this will probably make possible for her an accelerated involvement in the interweaving process.

NOW THAT SHE'S FEEDING ON THE EUCHARIST, IT'S TIME
FOR HER BAPTISM. FOR KATHERINE, JOINING ALL SAINTS
CHURCH IS HER MOMENT OF BAPTISM: WHETHER SHE'S
BEEN BAPTIZED BEFORE, SHE IS ABOUT TO BE IMMERSED
NOT IN WATER BUT IN THE LIFE OF THIS CONGREGATION.
IN HER NEW MEMBER PROCESS, SHE EXPERIENCES THE SAC-
RAMENT OF BELONGING, WHICH IS WHAT BAPTISM IS
ABOUT. THIS SACRAMENT IS ABOUT DYING AND RISING
AGAIN, ABOUT WHAT SHE'S GIVING UP AND WHAT SHE'S
TAKING ON. WHAT SHE'S GIVING UP IS A WAY OF LIFE THAT
BECAME GRAY DEATH FOR HER; STILL, THE LETTING GO WILL
NOT BE EASY. SO WHAT SHE'S TAKING ON WILL HAVE TO BE
COMFORTING AND FULL OF PROMISE FOR HER AND HER
CHILDREN. AS YOU BAPTIZE HER IN THIS NEW MEMBER PRO-
CESS, GIVE CAREFUL THOUGHT TO WHAT WILL PROVIDE
COMFORT TO HER, AND THE PROMISE OF AN ABUNDANT FU-
TURE. IMMERSE HER DEEPLY IN THIS SACRAMENT OF BE-
LONGING.

The New Members Class will perhaps be most effective if there
is a balanced emphasis on both the didactic and experiential aspects, between the content of the teaching and what happens for
people as they are taught. Obviously, the didactic dimension will involve the pastoral staff. But the experiential aspects may be the responsibility of highly-trained lay leadership.

Four objectives should be kept in mind in this regard:

A. Katherine should become a part of a regular small group (6-
10 persons), and she should meet, come to know at a deep level,
and be known by each of these persons. Highly trained leaders
should facilitate this kind of interpersonal mixing.

BY LEARNING TO LAUGH AND CRY WITH PEOPLE SHE CAN
TRUST, KATHERINE WILL FIND NOT ONLY PSYCHOLOGICAL
WELL-BEING, BUT ALSO THE FORGIVENESS FOR HER PAST
AND THE ACCEPTANCE OF WHO SHE IS WHICH WILL OPEN
THE DOOR OF HER SPIRITUAL JOURNEY.

B. These same leaders should help Katherine explore and process the Christian faith in a distinctly personal way. She should have
an opportunity to experience, both affectively and cognitively, God's
enormous caring for her, deep awareness of her, and the importance she has for God.

KATHERINE NEEDS A LANGUAGE WITH WHICH TO TALK
ABOUT ME, A LANGUAGE THAT IS TRUE BOTH TO WHO I AM
AND TO WHO SHE IS. SHE WILL NEED THOUGHTFUL TEACH-
ERS IN THIS PROCESS.

C. She should have an opportunity to emphasize the distinctive-
ness of her beliefs, as well as the doubts she may encounter in herself.

HELP HER TO SPELL EPISCOPALIAN WITH THE ALPHABET OF
HER OWN SOUL.

D. And when she has completed the class, she should know
each member of the ministerial staff by name, and they should
know her name. Moreover, she should feel that at least ten laypersons in the church know her well, care for her deeply, and are fully
aware of her unique situation.

REMEMBER, KATHERINE HAS BEEN ALONE. IN THIS EXPERI-
ENCE OF BAPTISM, HELP HER TO FIND THE FIRST MEMBERS
OF HER NEW FAMILY OF FAITH.

(6) First Year After Becoming A Member

I suggest that all persons in new member classes be strongly encouraged to maintain their involvement with each other during a
three-year period immediately following their reception into membership.

THROUGH THE YEAR OF THE EUCHARIST AND THE SACRA-
MENT OF BELONGING, KATHERINE HAS MOVED FROM THE
PARKING LOT INTO THE CHURCH: SHE IS NOW VERY MUCH A
PART OF THE ALL SAINTS FAMILY. NICELY DONE, FAITHFUL
FRIENDS. DURING THE NEXT FEW YEARS, I WANT YOU TO
MINISTER TO HER WITH TWO THOUGHTS IN MIND: TO EN-
RICH HER LIFE, AND TO EQUIP HER FOR MINISTRY. THE EN-
RICHING WILL REQUIRE EXCELLENT WORSHIP, A LOVING
COMMUNITY, AND HER DEEPENING CONVICTION THAT SHE
IS VALUED BY THIS CONGREGATION AND BY ME. TO EQUIP
HER, YOU WILL NEED TO TEACH HER *THE STORY*, AND HELP
HER FIND HER OWN GIFTS TO USE IN THE CONTINUING
STORY. THE DANGER IS THAT YOU WILL TAKE HER FOR
GRANTED: "AFTER ALL, SHE'S ONE OF US NOW." BUT I HAVE
PARTICULAR THINGS IN MIND FOR HER, THINGS THAT RE-

QUIRE OF YOU AS MUCH CARE NOW AS YOU GAVE TO HER IN THE BEGINNING.

The curriculum for the first year should be carefully designed to deepen her faith, motivate her outreach, and increase her involvement in the caring community.

The central aspect of this first-year experience should be the sense of togetherness the new members develop as a heterogenous group of Christian people. They should be encouraged to interweave themselves into the lives of as many of these persons as possible—even though there are significant differences in socio-economic class, race, educational background, occupation or profession, and length of involvement in the life of the church.

The formal curriculum for this first year might well include three courses—each lasting for 6-10 weeks. These might be:

A. The ten most critical aspects of our faith.

B. Ten programs of outreach to the world from which you may wish to choose one or two.

C. The fundamental qualities in the relationships of persons who are a part of the church of Jesus Christ.

(7) Second Year After Membership

While it will be important to provide multiple opportunities for these persons to be involved with one another, it will also be useful for them to begin to experience involvement with persons outside their own "entering class." During this second year these persons should be encouraged to be involved in at least one ongoing class each quarter of the year. Five such opportunities might be:

A. A study and prayer group consisting of intense Bible study and opportunity for deep praying about personal matters.

B. Time limited therapy group(s) for 8-10 persons lasting 20 sessions. These groups should be led by professional therapists within the membership, and the group should be structured to permit deep and caring involvement within the time limits set.

C. Three to five special weekend workshops should be held during the year for the treatment of problems and concerns involving family, teenagers, substance abuse, etc.

D. There should be at least one ongoing social group opportunity involving persons of varying marital status.

E. Out of this class there should be several outreach groups which include opportunity for personal relating and shared efforts to serve.

(8) Third Year After Membership

Throughout the first three years after a person becomes a member of the church, certain processes should be handled on a formal basis:

A. Each person should have a shepherd during the entire time.

B. Each person should be strongly encouraged to maintain regular involvement in one or more classes or groups at all times.

C. Each person should be assigned one member of the pastoral staff who contacts this person on a personal basis at least two or three times per year.

D. Each person should be reviewed at least annually by her shepherd and the relevant pastor in regard to how well she is being cared for and how fully she is involved in caring for others.

(9) Fourth Year After Membership

During the fourth year after membership, it may be well to treat these persons as though they were "upper division" in an educational institution. By now they should be ready to:

A. Be trained for special leadership positions in the church.

B. Be ready to assume responsibility for providing a highly personalized caring community for newcomers.

C. Be involved in giving generously and serving actively.

D. Be involved in a regular review of how well their needs for caring are being met on emotional, spiritual, and physical levels.

(10) Proceeding To Leadership

Katherine Simpson has now been involved with All Saints Church for five years. She is well known by scores of people in the church, and her special needs have been carefully assessed and attended to for sixty months. Her children are 15 and 13. Their lives have already been deeply influenced by their participation in classes at the church. Katherine is much more comfortable with her life, and there is no question in her mind about her value as a person and her worthwhileness as a member of her church.

> BEFORE I FORMED YOU IN THE WOMB, I KNEW YOU, AND BEFORE YOU WERE BORN I CONSECRATED YOU; I APPOINTED YOU AS A WITNESS." DURING THESE FIVE YEARS YOU, KATHERINE, HAVE LISTENED AND RESPONDED TO ME, AND YOU, DEAR CONGREGATION, HAVE PROVIDED FOR KATHERINE EXPERIENCES OF GRACE AND NURTURE. NOW, THIS FAR INTO HER JOURNEY, WE ARE READY FOR THE NEXT STEP: TO CALL YOU, KATHERINE, TO THAT MINISTRY FOR WHICH YOU HAVE BEEN PREPARING, BOTH BEFORE AND SINCE YOUR INTRODUCTION TO ALL SAINTS. YOU HAVE LISTENED TO AND LOVED YOUR WAY INTO THIS CONGREGATION'S LIFE; YOU HAVE LISTENED TO THE WORLD'S PAIN; AND YOU AND THE CONGREGATION HAVE LISTENED TO YOUR OWN INNER VOICES. OUT OF THIS HAS COME YOUR CALLING, THAT FOR WHICH "I APPOINTED YOU A WITNESS."

But if she is to further her growth, her continuing needs must be taken very seriously in a highly individualized way. If she has leadership skills, someone must care enough to assess those skills and encourage her to use them. If she has special talents in music and worship, leading Bible studies, reaching out to needy people, encouraging others to be involved in the life of the church, she needs to be trained and motivated to utilize every ounce of that potential.

Katherine Simpson came to All Saints Church because her life was gray. She felt unloved, unneeded, undirected. If she encountered a five-year process like the one described in this paper, the probability of her having become aware of and committed to her own unique gifts seems assured.

Perhaps she is a member of the vestry now—a far cry from that Sunday morning when she shook her way from Eagle Rock to Pasadena. She has been caringly woven into the life of a congregation, and her life, the lives of her children and their children, will be significantly richer because of it.

Interview Questions

Below are listed the questions used in the interviews done by the consultants studying the assimilation processes for the research from which this paper was written.

Context and Search

1. How did you first discover that this congregation existed?

2. If you first heard about this parish by being invited, who was it that invited you?

The pastor at that time   _____

A member of the church who was a stranger to you

A member of the church who was related to you _____

A member of the church who was a friend of yours

Other   _____

3. Had you attended a church of this denomination before?

4. Before going into the building, and before meeting the members, was there anything you found attractive about the place or intriguing about what you thought might go on in it?

5. What were you looking for in a church family or worship community?

6. What were your first impressions of the clergy (If there were more than one, describe each one)?

7. When you first came to the church, were you singled out or identified as a newcomer? How did this make you feel?

8. Did your family come to church with you?

9. Did anyone ever ask you what you were looking for in a church? How did it make you feel?

10. Were any of the following occurring near the time that you decided to "look into" this church?:

Recently changed residences   _____

Recently married   _____

Recently had a child   _____

Recently had experienced a major life crisis   _____

Recently had a significant faith experience   _____

Did coming to church have anything to do with the above?

Testing, Returning, Joining

11. Who were the people that helped you move deeper into the life of the parish?

12. When did you *feel* accepted in this congregation?

How long did it take?

Did something happen that made you *feel* accepted?

13. When did you have your first conversation with the pastor?

14. Did a lay person or lay team visit you in your home after you first attended the church?

15. What, if any, were some of the surprises you experienced while getting acquainted with this congregation?

16. Is there anything that happened that almost kept you from becoming active in this congregation?

17. How long did you attend before joining?

18. How did you learn the history of the parish?

19. Can you describe any experience you've had since becoming a part of the church wherein you felt uncomfortable, awkward, or put off? What happened?

20. How many of your close friends are members of this parish?

21. What has been the most moving and satisfying personal experience in this parish?

22. How were you made aware of the church's programs and activities?

Sunday Announcements   _____

Church Bulletin   _____

Church Newsletter   _____

Orientation Program   _____

Personal invitation by parish staff   _____

Invitation by a lay person who was a friend   _____

Invitation by a lay person who was a stranger _____

Other   _____

23. How did you become involved in your first activity?

Personal initiative   _____

Invitation by parish staff   _____

Invitation by a lay person who was a friend   _____

Invitation by a lay person who was a stranger _____

24. What role did the clergy play in helping you become a member?

Going Deeper

25. Where are you growing and being challenged in you life now?

26. As a newcomer, did you get any sense of what it means to grow in the Christian faith from the pastor or lay leaders in the congregation?

27. As a newcomer, had the congregation communicated to you as to what it expects of you as a member?

28. Did anyone communicate with you the church's expectations with regard to Sunday worship attendance?

29. How were you made aware of financial responsibilities to the church?

30. Did the congregation offer to train you to identify and to recruit other potential members?

31. Are there different expectations in this parish for the participation of men and women?

32. Does this parish require certain beliefs or attitudes from people who are joining?

33. As a newcomer, did the parish invite you to take on any personal spiritual disciplines on your own or with others?

34. Does the parish have standards that it communicates to its members about appropriate ways Christians should express their faith?

35. Does there seem to be any differentiation in the programs in the church for persons who "are just getting started" on their Christian journey and those for persons who have been exploring their faith for a longer time?

36. What programs or resources does your church have which help people at various levels explore their faith more deeply?

    Retreats   _____

    Prayer Groups   _____

    Courses   _____

    Library   _____

New Member Assimilation Rating Scale

The following rating scale has been devised to assist your congregation assess its effectiveness in the new member incorporation process.

We recommend using it with your chief decision making body or your new member development committee. When used with a group or committee, have each individual complete the survey independently. Later, when the committee gathers, have each member share their assessment on each question with the group, followed by a discussion of the same until a group consensus is reached on each question.

The value of this process will be determined by the candor level of both individuals and the group discussion. For your congregation to increase its ability to incorporate members well, your committee will first need to get a clear fix on your present process, with its strengths and weaknesses.

It's difficult to improve a parish process until there is an agreement on what is actually taking place. We hope you all will have fun with the process as well as learn a whole lot about your parish and each other. The scoring sheet is on page 110.

I. Attracting/Recruiting

a) A message of faith, hope and love is proclaimed on a regular basis at our parish by both clergy and lay people

2	4	8	12	16	20
Untrue			Partially True		True

b) The good news of the Gospel is lived out in the way people relate to each other in the parish

2	4	8	12	16	20
Untrue			Partially True		True

c) I am pleased with the variety of ways our congregation attracts newcomers to the parish

1	2	3	4	5	6
Untrue		Partially True			True

d) I am pleased with the positive image our congregation has in its immediate community because of the various ways we serve the community

1	2	3	4	5	6
Untrue		Partially true			True

e) Our members regularly invite their non-churched friends and family members to attend this church with them

1	2	3	4	5	6
Untrue		Partially true			True

f) Add 2 points to your score if you have any of the following things going for you in attracting newcomers

_____ Bells, carillons

_____ A community newsletter

_____ Weekly newspaper, radio, T. V. ads

_____ Attractive, inviting buildings

_____ Attractive signs on the church exterior that communicate times of services and Sunday church school

_____ Day care center/parochial school

g) Add 2 points for every non-parish community group that uses your facilities on a regular basis, i.e. Boy Scout troop, Alcoholic Anonymous, etc.

_____ _____

_____ _____

II. Testing

h) Our congregation easily recognizes visitors and people go out of their way to make them feel accepted and welcome

1	2	3	4	5	6
Untrue		Partially true			True

i) It is rare that a visitor leaves our congregation without someone getting a name and address for followup purposes

1	2	3	4	5	6
Untrue		Partially true			True

j) Our congregation has a coffee hour/social gathering following Sunday services at which time visitors are approached warmly by regular attenders of the parish

1	2	3	4	5	6
Untrue		Partially true			True

k) When it is obvious that visitors are lost in our congregation's liturgy, we have persons in the congregation who will quietly slip in beside them to assist them to participate

1	2	3	4	5	6
Untrue		Partially true			True

III. Returning/Affiliating

Give your congregation the prescribed points for each of the following (note: count both 10 and 6 if your lay visitation team visits within a week that follows Sunday attendance)

l) _____(10)   Lay visitation teams that call on visitors in the week that follows their Sunday attendance

m)_____(6)   Lay visitation teams that call on visitors within a month of their Sunday attendance

n) _____(10)   A staff member who makes calling on parish visitors a priority

o) _____(6)   A printed brochure/folder which describes the nature of your congregation, and outlines parish programs offered

p) _____(4)   A letter of welcome that is mailed to all parish visitors within a week

q) _____(6)   A clean, attractive nursery which is attended by warm, caring people

r) _____(10)   A quality Sunday church school for all ages

s) _____(6)   An active youth group

t) _____(6)   An active young adult group

u) _____(6)   A couples' group

v) _____(6)   Mid-week prayer/Bible study groups

w)_____(10)   A variety of small groups (study, service, or decision making groups) which are open to receiving
newcomers into their midst

x) _____(10)   Periodic short orientation seminars for visitors as-
sisting them to become familiar with the parish's
liturgy, symbols, architecture (other than new
member class.)

IV. Joining

y) Our congregation requires all potential new members to attend
new member classes of 4 sessions or more before joining

2	4	6	8	10	12
Untrue		Partially true			True

z) Our congregation makes clear to newcomers what is expected of
them as members.

2	4	6	8	10	12
Untrue		Partially true			True

aa) Our congregation invites joiners to observe certain personal or
family spiritual disciplines on their own to support their growth and
development as members, i.e. grace at meals, private prayer, Bible/
devotional readings, etc.

1	2	3	4	5	6
Untrue		Partially true			True

bb) Our congregation publicly receives all joiners into membership
at a service of worship through a special liturgical event.

1	2	3	4	5	6
Untrue		Partially true			True

cc) In addition to celebrating new members joining at a service,
there is an additional event in the parish to honor joiners and have
them meet several other members, i.e. potluck dinner, luncheon
with the pastor, etc.

1	2	3	4	5	6
Untrue		Partially true			True

V. Going Deeper

Our congregation has a coordinator of lay volunteers or designated person who interviews joiners to ascertain

dd) their gifts and talents

1	2	3	4	5	6
Untrue			Partially true		True

ee) their interest in specific parish activities

1	2	3	4	5	6
Untrue			Partially true		True

ff) their desire for growth opportunities

1	2	3	4	5	6
Untrue			Partially true		True

gg) their ministry in the world and ways in which the parish might support them in that ministry

1	2	3	4	5	6
Untrue			Partially true		True

hh) Once or twice a year our parish sponsors a gifts identification event to help members become clearer about their call to ministry and the ways the parish might assist them in that ministry through prayer, growth events, service opportunities

1	4	8	12	16	20
Untrue			Partially true		True

ii) Our parish has a person who regularly monitors the involvement of lay volunteers to ensure prevention of burnout, e.g. watches overuse of the same faithful leaders

1	3	5	7	9	11
Untrue			Partially true		True

jj) Our parish consistently supports the notion that lay ministry is what Christians do in the community or world and that parish activities are there to support these ministries

1	3	5	7	9	11
Untrue			Partially true		True

VI. Being Sent

kk) Our parish consistently challenges and trains new members to work on new member ministries

1	4	7	10	13	16
Untrue			Partially true		True

ll) Our parish consistently encourages all parish members to invite their friends and family members to accompany them to church

1	4	7	10	13	16
Untrue			Partially true		True

mm) The New Member Development Committee is given freedom to request all other committees in the church assist them in their task, e.g. have property committee post better signs, train ushers in new member greetings, have music and worship committee more effectively gear services to newcomers, etc.

1	4	7	10	13	16
Untrue			Partially true		True

New Member Assimilation Rating Scale

I. Attracting/Recruiting

a) _____

b) _____

c) _____

d) _____

e) _____

f) _____

g) _____

II. Testing

h) _____

i) _____

j) _____

k) _____

III. Returning/Affiliating

l) _____

m) _____

n) _____

o) _____

p) _____

q) _____

r) _____

IV. Joining

y) _____

z) _____

aa) _____

bb) _____

cc) _____

V. Going Deeper

dd) _____

ee) _____

ff) _____

gg) _____

hh) _____

ii) _____

jj) _____

VI. Being Sent

kk) _____

ll) _____

mm) _____

Total _____

Total _____

Total I - III _____

Total IV - V _____

Grand Total _____

Good Score for Corporate Church	180 or higher
Good Score for Program Church	85 or higher
Good Score for Pastoral Church	55 or higher
Fair Score for Corporate Church	150 or higher
Fair Score for Program Church	60 or higher
Fair Score for Pastoral Church	40 or higher
Poor Score for Corporate Church	130 or higher
Poor Score for Program Church	45 or higher
Poor Score for Pastoral Church	30 or higher

BIBLIOGRAPHY

Akeman, Gene, "The Pilgrimage of Faith," *Action Information*, The Alban Institute, Inc., September/October, 1986.

Anderson, James D. and Jones, Ezra Earl, *The Management of Ministry*, San Francisco: Harper & Row, 1978.

Biersdorf, John E., *Hunger for Experience: Vital Religious Communities in America*, New York: The Seabury Press, Inc., 1975.

————*Healing of Purpose: God's Call to Discipleship*, Nashville: Abingdon, 1985.

Byers, Harold H.; Matthew, John C.; Ploth, Richard E.; Rounseville, Margaret Anne; Vogan, David and Welker, David J., "Enabling Middle Judicatories to Assist Congregations in Communities Where There Appears to be Little Opportunity for Numerical Growth." Unpublished report, Congregational Development Program, Ministries With Congregations, The Program Agency, The United Presbyterian Church, USA, 1979.

Dudley, Carl, *Where Have All Our People Gone?* New York: Pilgrim Press, 1979.

————"How can a small church grow?" *Christian Ministry*, July 1977.

Dunkin, Steve, *Church Advertising: A Practical Guide*, ed. by Lyle E. Schaller (Creative Leadership Series), Nashville: Abingdon, 1982.

Dvorscak, James, "A Better Way to Say Hello: Welcoming New Parishioners from Other Parishes," *Action Information*, The Alban Institute, Inc., March/April, 1987.

Fowler, Jim and Keen, Sam, *Life Maps: Conversations on the Journey of Faith*, Waco: Word, 1979.

Freeman, Forster, *Readiness for Ministry Through Spiritual Direction*, Washington: The Alban Institute, Inc., 1986.

Hoge, Dean R., *Converts, Dropouts, Returnees: A Study of Religious Change Among Catholics*, Washington: United States Catholic Conference and New York: The Pilgrim Press, 1981.

Gigee, Brian K., "Creating Intentional Hospitality," *Church Management— The Clergy Journal*, July, 1986.

Gribbon, R. T., *Half The Congregation: Ministry with 18 to 40 Year Olds*, Washington: The Alban Institute, Inc., 1984.

————*Thirty Year Olds and the Church: Ministry with the Baby Boom Generation*, Washington: The Alban Institute, Inc., 1981.

————*When People Seek the Church*, Washington: The Alban Institute, Inc. 1982.

Grierson, Denham, *Transforming A People of God*, Melbourne: The Joint Board of Christian Education of Australia and New Zealand, 1984.

Hoge, Dean R. and Roozen, David A. (ed), *Understanding Church Growth and Decline: 1950-1958*, New York: The Pilgrim Press, 1979.

Hopewell, James F., *Congregation: Stories and Structures*, Philadelphia: Fortress, 1987.

Hunter III, George G., *The Contagious Congregation: Frontiers in Evangelism and Church Growth*, Nashville: Abingdon, 1979.

Hunter, Kent R., *Your Church Has Personality*, Nashville: Abingdon, 1985.

Johnson, Roger A., *Congregations as Nurturing Communities: A Study of Nine Congregations of the Lutheran Church in America*, Division for Parish Services, Lutheran Church in America, 1979.

Mann, Alice B., *Incorporation of New Members in the Episcopal Church: A Manual for Clergy and Lay Leaders*, Philadelphia: Ascension Press, 1983.

McGavran, Donald and Arn, Win C., *How to Grow A Church*, Glendale: G/L Publications, 1973.

McSwain, Larry, "Principles for Effective Church Growth," Metropolitan Missions Department Home Missions Board, June 1, 1981.

Perry, Edward, "Where Are the People?," *Action Information*, The Alban Institute, September 1977.

————*Ten Steps for Church Growth*, San Francisco: Harper & Row, 1977.

Rauff, Edward A., *Why People Join the Church: An Exploratory Study*, New York: The Pilgrim Press, 1979.

Riser, Steven Craig, *A Strategy for the Assimilation of New Members into the Life and Ministry of a Local Congregation*, Doctoral Dissertation, Columbia Theological Seminary, 1981.

Roof, Wade Clark and McKinney, William, *American Mainline Religion*, New Brunswick: Rutgers University Press, 1987.

Rothauge, Arlin J., *Sizing Up A Congregation: for New Member Ministry*, Seabury Professional Services.

Rothauge, Arlin J., *Reshaping a Congregation for a New Future*, New York: The Episcopal Church Center, 1985.

Saarinen, Martin F., *The Life Cycle of a Congregation*, Washington: The Alban Institute, Inc., 1986.

Savage, John S., *The Apathetic and Bored Church Member*, L.E.A.D. Consultants, P.O. Box 311, Pittsford, NY 14534.

Schaller, Lyle E., *Assimilating New Members*, ed by Lyle E. Schaller, Creative Leadership Series), Nashville: Abingdon, 1978.

————"Trade-Offs in Church Growth," *Presbyterian Survey*, April 1985.

————"The Unraveling of Tradition," *The Lutheran*, January 16, 1985.

————"Where are the Visitors?," *Church Management—The Clergy Journal*, April 1984.

Thomas, Lloyd J., "Hazards and Signposts on Spiritual Journeys," *Journal of Religion and the Applied Behavioral Sciences*, Winter, 1987.

Wagner, Peter C., *Church Growth: State of the Art*, Wheaton: Tyndale House, 1986.

Westerhoff, John. *Will Our Children Have Faith?* New York: Seabury, 1976.

Willimon, William H., "Making Christians in a Secular World," *The Christian Century*, October 22, 1986.

The Alban Institute:
an invitation to membership

The Alban Institute, begun in 1974, believes that the congregation is essential to the task of equipping the people of God to minister in the church and the world. A multi-denominational membership organization, the Institute provides on-site training, educational programs, consulting, research, and publishing for hundreds of churches across the country.

The Alban Institute invites you to be a member of this partnership of laity, clergy and executives—a partnership that brings together people who are raising important questions about congregational life and people who are trying new solutions, making new discoveries, finding a new way of getting clear about the task of ministry. The Institute exists to provide you with the kinds of information and resources you need to support your ministries.

Join us now and enjoy these benefits:

Publications Discounts

Discounts on Training and Continuing Education

Research Reports and Occasional Papers

Inside Information

Action Information, a highly respected journal published 6 times a year, to keep you up to date on current issues and trends.

Write us for more information about how to join The Alban Institute.

The Alban Institute, Inc.
4125 Nebraska Avenue NW
Washington, DC 20016